CW01095577

# Jean Restayn

# Tiger I on the Eastern Front

**Histoire & Collections**

# Tiger I on the Eastern Front

## Contents

*Caption of front cover illustration:*
**Tiger I of the 502. s. Panzer-Abteilung, Spring-Summer 1943.**
*(Author's illustration)*

*Caption of back cover illustration:*
**Tiger A 21 belonged to the 9th company/ III. Abteilung of the "Grossdeutschland" Division. It took part in the fighting along the Rollbahn in June 1944, which cost the Red Army 70 tanks.**
*(Author's illustration)*

This umpteenth book on the Tiger does not claim to be exhaustive. It presents the different Tiger I units used on the Eastern front, in a clear and chronological manner. In order to do this, a majority of unpublished photographs have been used. They all give a host of interesting or unpublished details, as much for the model-maker as for the historian.

Certain photographs, already known without captions or with incorrect captions, are also shown in this book. They will certainly give the specialists a few surprises. Finally, the illustrations and the insignia details which also illustrate the book give some colour to this rather dark period of history.

*Jean Restayn*

# Introduction

*Above.*
**A Tiger of the s.Pz-Abt 501, hidden behind an isba, points its gun at the target.**
*(BA)*

*Left.*
**A second Tiger on its left advances through what was once a peaceful village.**
*(BA)*

*Below.*
**Once through the village, Tiger 231 covers a third tank, ahead on its left.**
*(BA)*

*Below.*
**The distance separating the machines is around at least one hundred metres. Reality has nothing to do with what we are shown in war films.**
*(BA)*

*Bottom right.*
**At least 13 shell cases can be counted on this shot. The use of the slightest gradient was often beneficial and added to the crew's safety.**
*(BA)*

Above.
**Tiger No. 111 of s.Pz-Abt.501 crossing a bridge named after** *Major* **Loewe, killed on 23rd December 1943. He was the commander of the battalion at the time.**
*(BA)*

*Right.*
**The first unit sign of Battalion 501, only used in North Africa**
*(Author's illustration)*

Formed on 10th May 1942 at Erfurt with elements from the 501 and 502 s.Pz- Jäger Kompanie, it fought from the end of November 1942 in Tunisia, with first one then two companies. After its surrender in North Africa, the battalion was reformed on 17th September 1943 at Paderborn with three companies. It fought on the Eastern Front, to the north-east of Minsk, then in the Krakow sector and finally to the east of Prague.

On 15th January 1945, it was renamed s.Pz-Abt. 424 and fought until its disbanding in the Vistula sector. On 11th February, the remaining tanks were used to form the s.Pz-Abt. 512 (Jagdtiger).

From November 1942 to February 1945, the battalion destroyed 450 enemy tanks, of which 150 in Tunisia. The s.Pz-Abt.501 (424) used not less than 120 Tiger Is and 45 Tiger IIs during the whole conflict.

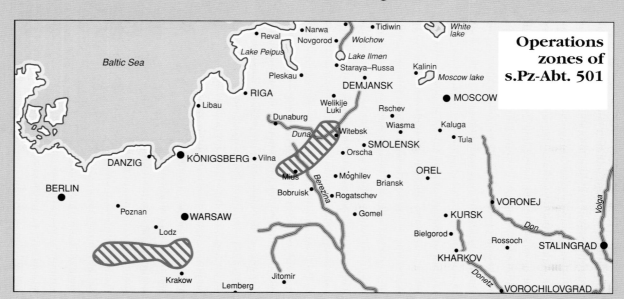

**Operations zones of s.Pz-Abt. 501**

*Right.*
**At the beginning of December 1943, the Tigers were loaded at Mailly-le-Camp (France), destination: the Eastern Front. This machine from the 1st Company No. 114 is shod with transport tracks, the *Verladenketten*.**
*(BA)*

*Below.*
**Mailly-le-Camp, December 1943. An eighteen-tonne SdKfz 9/1 equipped with a 6-tonne crane was an integral part of the Tiger battalions' maintenance workshop at the time.**
*(WS)*

**Tiger of the s.Pz.-Abt. 501, the company commander's machine. The battalion was wholly committed in mid-December 1943 in the Witebsk sector. In five days, the Tigers destroyed 81 Russian tanks for the loss of four of theirs.**
**At the time, the tanks were already covered with Zimmerit. The figures on the turret were simply outlined with black on the camouflage background, with yellow ochre added for better visibility. After a year of fighting, the battalion had lost a total of 45 Tiger Is. In mid-July 1944, it received the new Tiger IIs.**
*(Author's illustration)*

10th December 1943, unloading at Bialistok. Changing the tracks was an operation that was detested by the maintenance crews, especially in bad weather. This Tiger displays No. 302 on the turret and the tractor's registration number is 1982.
*(WS)*

*Right.*
**Tiger No. 111 of the 1st Company at the inauguration of the "Major Loewe" bridge. Note the traces of fighting as well as the flaking Zimmerit and the number painted on the steel.**
*(BA)*

*Below.*
**Another scene dating from 21 March 1944, at the moment of the inauguration. Notice the relatively good weather for an early Russian Spring!**
*(BA)*

*Generaloberst* **Lindemann presiding over the inauguration, keeping his feet warm on the engine hatches of Tiger 111.**
*(BA)*

*Left.*
The bridge seems particularly solid and can obviously take the 56 tonnes of the Tiger (plus the weight of the General!). Bridges were only crossed by one Tiger at a time.
*(BA)*

*Right.*
Tank No. 311 (3rd Company). One of the crew members took this photo in December 1944 in the Witebsk sector.
*(WS)*

*Below.*
The crew of Tiger 332 posing on their white-speckled machine.This tank is showing some wear and tear, such as a missing side mud-guard.
*(WS)*

A Tiger I of the 2nd Company of the s.Pz.-Abt. 501. The shape of the figures on the turret is typical of the unit. All the Tigers of the unit have rubber-lined wheels. The machine took part in Operation Hubertus during the first half of March 1944, breaking through the Soviet encirclement in the Nipinzy-Sabory region.
*(Author's illustration)*

Hairdressing saloon improvised on a Tiger, the 88 cannon used as a seat. The ultimate in luxury is the use of a mirror and a towel, as well as the scissors.
*(BA)*

*Top left.*
Tiger 331 sporting a very washed-out camouflage. This part of the Winter seems to have been more humid than cold, which explains the crews' relatively light clothes.
*(WS)*

*Left.*
Tiger 321 showing a missing road wheel just behind the drive sprocket-wheel. Mud collecting at this point could freeze and hamper the vehicle's mobility.
*(WS)*

*Opposite page, top left.*
**As for 111, this shot of Tiger 211 shows the numbers painted directly on to the white camouflage at the rear of the Rommelkiste. Note the racks for the jerrycans at rear left, which were typical of the unit.**
*(BA)*

*Opposite page, top tight.*
**Operation Hubertus in mid-March 1944, in the Siwizkje sector. Tiger 332, showing several impacts on the front plate, passes another Tiger in the unit.**
*(BA)*

*Left.*
s. Panzer-Abteilung 501's unit sign in North Africa.
*(Author's illustration)*

*Below.*
**Shot taken during Operation Hubertus. In the background is a Panzer IV of the 20. Panzerdivision.**
*(BA)*

*Above.*
**This photo is of particular interest as it shows the special Winter headgear of a Tiger crewman chatting with a member of the "Hermann Göring" Division. In certain books, this machine is mis-attributed to the "Grossdeutschland" division early in 1943 at Kharkov. This is wrong, as established by the presence of Zimmerit on the tank.**
*(BA)*

*Left.*
**A Tiger from the 501st in the Russian immensity. In order to avoid attracting artillery fire, Tigers had to change position frequently.** *(BA)*

*Below.*
**A Tiger of the 3rd company of the s.Pz.-Abt. 501 during Spring 1944. The figures are outlined in red on the sides and rear of the turret. The month of April was good for the unit as spare parts were available in sufficient numbers to overhaul almost thirty tanks... But the fighting in the following months reduced the unit's hopes to nothing, for the second time.**
*(Author's illustration)*

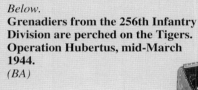

*Below.*
**Grenadiers from the 256th Infantry Division are perched on the Tigers. Operation Hubertus, mid-March 1944.**
*(BA)*

*Left.*
**Two Tigers from the 3rd company, 314 with 312 in the background, seem to be protecting their *Gulaschkanone* (mobile field kitchen).**
*(BA)*

*Below.*
**Artillerymen from the 256th Artillery regiment gather round a Tiger of the 501st, which seems to be watching over their position.**
*(BA)*

*Below, left.*
**Re-arming a Tiger of the 2nd company, the 211. Note the impressive number of shells that the Tiger could carry. Here also, the jerrycan rack is perfectly visible.**
*(BA)*

*Left.*
**With the coming of Spring, the machines were overhauled and their white camouflage cleaned up. These three are from the 3rd company.**
*(WS)*

*Right.*
**Another view of the same hangar with No 314 in the background. For some strange reason the numbers are painted in white. The foremost Tiger is equipped with Feiffel filters, which was rare for the unit.** *(WS)*

12

13

Formed on 25th May 1942, it was the first operational Tiger battalion and was sent in August to the Leningrad front to be tried out under combat conditions. On 21st September, it was badly used and suffered its first losses on terrain unsuited to tank movement, in the Torlowo sector. The 502nd took part in the various battles of Lake Ladoga in the Leningrad sector.

After re-structuring, it was made up to three companies. Fighting continued in the northern sector of the Leningrad-Pleskau-Memel-Königsberg front. The unit was one of the most formidable, with a tally of 1,400 Soviet tanks destroyed for 105 Tiger Is and 8 Tiger IIs used. Amongst its aces were *Oberleutnant* Carius with 150 enemy tanks destroyed (170 according to some), *Hauptmann* Bölter with 144, and *Feldwebel* Kerscher with 100.

*Above.*
**Tiger 332 of the 502nd during the Winter 1943-44. This shot gives a good impression of the tank's undeniable strength. The sacks piled up on the sides serve as bedding for the crew.**
*(BA)*

*Inset.*
**Unit sign of s.Pz-Abt. 502.**
*(Author's illustration)*

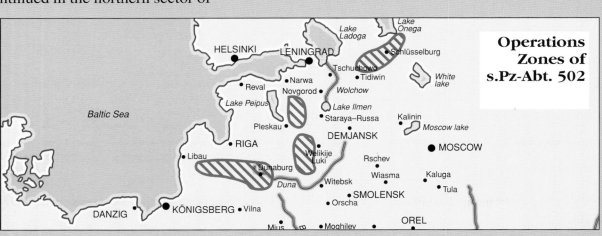

Operations Zones of s.Pz-Abt. 502

# eilung 502

*Right.*
One of the first four Tigers of the unit at Fallingbostel in August 1942, here No. 100. Note the front mud-guard of the first series tanks and the absence of side mud-guards. *(WS)*

*Below.*
One of the first operational Tigers in the conflict belonged to the 1st company of the s.Pz.-Abt. 502. The battalion fought alongside the 170th Infantry division at the end of September 1942 in the Totolowo sector against the elite 2nd Russian Army. The camouflage is simply green on a grey base. On the front is the famous mammoth, the battalion's symbol. At this time the s.Pz.-Abt. 502 only had 7 Tigers. Note the absence of Feiffel filters, exhaust pipe fairings, and side mud-guards. The front mudguards are from the first series. *(Author's illustration)*

*Below.*
Another machine from the same unit, No. 112. It has the same characteristics as No. 100 and like its mate, is fitted with transport tracks. *(WS)*

*Inset.*
s.Pz-Abt. 502's unit sign, displayed throughout 1942, until the end of Winter. *(Author's illustration)*

The unit's insignia is painted large on the back of the turret and small on the front plate, to the right of the radio-operator's station. *(WS)*

15

*Above.*
**Panzer III No. 116 in an awkward position, abandoned. This photo was taken by the enemy and the tank was lost during fighting in the Winter of 1942-43 before Leningrad.** *(G. Gorokhoff)*

*Right.*
**Tiger under repair, Winter 1942-43. The machine belongs to the first series and has fixation points for the side mud-guards. Note the impact on the 80mm armour.** *(BA)*

*Left.*
**A tank crew talking in front of its machine during the Winter of 1942-43. The tank is from the succeeding series as the bolts for fixing the side mud-guards are clearly visible.** *(WS)*

*Below left.*
**A typical unit camouflage in February 1943. The battalion only had 5 operational Tigers at this period.** *(WS)*

*Below.*
**No. 1 has another variant of the camouflage. The Rommelkiste is grey.** *(WS)*

*Left.*
**Tiger No. 4 camouflaged in undergrowth during February 1943. At this period, the unit only had five Tigers, numbered 1 - 5.**
*(WS)*

*Above.*
**February 1943, a column of two Tigers and at least one Pz III during the Battle of Lake Ladoga.**
*(WS)*

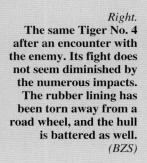

*Right.*
**The same Tiger No. 4 after an encounter with the enemy. Its fight does not seem diminished by the numerous impacts. The rubber lining has been torn away from a road wheel, and the hull is battered as well.**
*(BZS)*

*Above.*
**Splendid shot of Tiger No. 2, from the first series, in the Spring of 1943. Note the absence of fixation screws for the side mud-guards. The number was soon to be changed to a two-digit number to give the impression of larger numbers.**
*(ECPA)*

*Right.*
**This Tiger without number is in countryside typical of the Leningrad area.**
*(ECPA)*

*Right.*
**Summer 1943, Tiger from the 1st company. In change-over periods, there wasn't even time to paint the numbers on the machines.**
*(ECPA)*

*Below.*
**At the beginning of 1943, s.Pz.-Abt. 502 only had 5 Tigers left. Two of these, including No. 3 illustrated here, were the survivors of the nine tanks delivered in Autumn 1942. From 21st September 1942 to 18th February 1943, they destroyed 107 Soviet tanks. This Tiger is one of the very first vehicles delivered (chassis number 250005), recognisable by the lack of side bolts for the mud-guards. The Feiffel filters are not mounted.**
*(Author's illustration)*

*Left.*
**Spring 1943, Tiger No. 1 operating in completely deserted countryside. At this period the battalion was reduced to a company and had only 14 tanks.**
*(BA)*

*Above, left.*
**Tiger 01 again, seen from the other side. Note the two wheels missing on the left side, owing to a lack of spare parts. In the background undergrowth lurks Tiger No. 21.**
*(BA)*

*Above.*
**The results are revealing, as demonstrated by these two KV-1Ss destroyed a couple of days beforehand.**
*(BA)*

*Opposite page, top.*
**Tiger No. 14 of s.Pz-Abt. 502. The tank seems to have been over-greased because of the heavy, humid northern climate. *(WS)***

*Opposite page, bottom.*
**Ex-Tiger No. 3 of December 1942 became No. 14 in the spring of 1943 and No. 113 in summer 1943. This tank was a veteran indeed! *(BA)***

*Above.*
**Tiger No. 21 in firing position. The fighting was particularly deadly in this sector as the s.Pz-Abt. 502 was the only tank unit available on this part of the front.**
*(BA)*

*Right.*
**Tiger 21 changing position after a firing sequence. Note the speckled camouflage and the turret number sometimes drawn with chalk.**
*(BA)*

*Above.*
**The same No. 113 showing the same marks, in a little Russian village. The civilian population suffered as much within Leningrad as in the neighbouring countryside.** *(BA)*

*Right.*
**Note the missing number for the 1st company on the back of this vehicle. The same detail can be noted for the rest of the company.**
*(BA)*

*Below..*
**Tank No. 134 also seems to be a veteran because of its lack of side mud-guards.**
*(BA)*

*Opposite page, top.*
**Tiger No. 232 in a moonscape, in full action. Note the BT 7 and in the background, a destroyed KV 1. A second Tiger is just behind 232.**
*(BF)*

*Opposite page.*
**Tank No. 133 well camouflaged with its cannon pointed towards five o'clock. Behind it is a 4.5 tonne Büssing crane-lorry, used for lifting Tiger engines.**
*(BA)*

*Opposite page, far right.*
**July 1943, a broken-down Tiger taken in tow by at least three 18-tonne SdKfz 9 tractors. The Tiger belongs to the 2nd company, tank commander Brand.**
*(WS)*

This tank is the ex-No. 3 (see on page 19) of the s.Pz.-Abt. 502 . At the beginning of Spring, the Tigers were repainted sand yellow. The markings were also changed and the white 3 became 14. The side bolts were mounted to receive the mud-guards, but the lack of spare parts prevented this job from being finished. This type of finish is, in our opinion, the most interesting for modellers.
*(Author's illustration)*

*Left.*
With the 3rd company, *Hauptfeldwebel* Piedcs' tank, who was also the *Kompaniefeldwebel.*
(WS)

*Below.*
Tank No. 231 of the 2nd company. The cross on a black square is characteristic of this unit.
(WS)

*Opposite page, top left.*
Lt. Carius' Tiger 213. As a Tiger ace, he finished the war with 150 victories, 170 according to some.
(WS)

*Below.*
Summer 1943, Tiger 312 passes No. 322. Note the difference in the style of the numbers. 322 in white seems to be the exception.
(BZS)

*Left.*
Tiger 224. As on all the machines of this company, the camouflage is almost nonexistent. The cross on a black background is perfectly visible.
(KM)

Form-ation sign of s. Panzer-Abteilung 502 from the Spring of 1943.
*(Author's illustration)*

*Above.*
**Tiger 221 had less luck, seen here damaged by a direct hit on the left side of the hull. The photograph was taken by Russian elite troops ; the machine was sent back to the USSR and exposed there.**
*(G. Gorokhoff)*

*Right.*
**Another interesting crew uniform. Summer 1943.** *(WS)*

*Left.*
Tiger 233. The insignia is scarcely visible on this machine. The box - presumably for tools - on the front suggests that the tank is far from the front-line. *(WS)*

*Above.*
Two interesting details in this photo taken in July 1943: the insignia and the chassis number 250256 of Tiger 312. It was destroyed a year later.
*(BA)*

This Tiger (chassis number 250005), which was originally No. 113 then 3 then 14 (see pages 19 and 23), returned to being 113, the rest of its story is unfortunately unknown as all trace of it was lost towards the end of Spring 1944. The Rommelkiste has been replaced by a new box, the exhaust pipe fairings, the side and rear mud-guards are missing. The grey base paint can be seen occasionally under the sand yellow.
*(Author's illustration)*

*Above.*
**Tiger from the 2nd company during the Newel battles, Winter of 1943-44.**
*(BA)*

*Right.*
**Infantry hiding behind a Tiger from the 2nd company. This was in fact dangerous as the tanks attracted concentrated fire from the enemy.**
*(BA)*

A Tiger of the 2nd company of the s.Pz.-Abt. 502 in February 1944. The 204 was one of the extra tanks in the battalion. In fact, certain Tiger units had a number of tanks in excess of the quota. At the end of February 1944, the battalion had 71 Tigers. At the same time the s.Pz.-Abt. 503, 507, and 509 had respectively 69, 56, and 58 Tigers. This was due to transfers from units re-training on Tiger IIs or the delivery of the last machines of production runs. Tiger production reached its peak between January and May 1944, and ceased in August 1944.
*(Author's illustration)*

*Top right.*
**The victorious tank crew seems proud of its score.**
*(BA)*

*Left.*
**Tiger from the 1st company during the Newel bridgehead battles. On the photograph the 22 victory rings on the barrel are not visible but it is the same machine.**
*(BA)*

*Right.*
**Autumn 1943, in the Newel sector. Tiger 224 is trying to get another Tiger out, even though such a manoeuvre was forbidden.**
*(WS)*

*Below.*
**Another Tiger towing a comrade in difficulty. The diversity of Winter camouflage patterns is apparent.**
*(BA)*

*Right.*
**Tiger 312 No. 250256 already well-known, with a greenish camouflage. There are at least three road wheels missing on the side. The tank is being towed past a destroyed T 34 model 43.**
*(BA)*

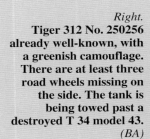

*Right.*
This shot through the windshield of a vehicle shows tank 201 which has lost its track on the right-hand side. The zebra-type camouflage is particularly interesting.
(BA)

*Below.*
A Tiger from the 2nd company passes through a burning village during a counter-attack, Winter 1943-44.
(BA)

*Above.*
A horse confronted with the 600 horsepower of a Tiger from the 1st company. But it was often the simplest means of transport which allowed sophisticated machines to be maintained.
(BA)

*Left.*
This photograph, dated 6th January 1944 during the fighting in the region of the Newel, shows Tiger No. 101 (white figures), well camouflaged.
(BA)

31

*Below.*
***Oberleutnant*** **Schiller and** *Leutnant* **Carius on 4th May 1944. Carius was decorated that day with the Knight's Cross of the Iron Cross. Carius is still alive, living in the Saar where he runs a chemist's, "The Tiger Chemist's". No comment!**
*(WS)*

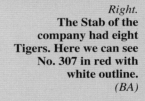

*Below.*
**Tiger 207 in February 1944. The Schwer Panzer-Abteilung 502 had 70 Tigers at the time, a record number for this unit. Note the flaking Zimmerit.**
*(BA)*

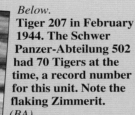

*Right.*
**The Stab of the company had eight Tigers. Here we can see No. 307 in red with white outline.**
*(BA)*

*Opposite page, right.*
**Summer 1944. Since the beginning of the year, the new Tigers were covered with Zimmerit.**
*(WS)*

*Above.*
**Tiger 217.** Companies sometimes fielded 29 tanks each, which explains such high numbers.
*(BA)*

A Tiger of the 3rd company of the s.Pz.-Abt. 502 in the Spring of 1944. At this time, the 3rd company was committed alongside the 1st in the Pleskau sector. Fighting there was very heavy and a lot of the 1 400 tanks and 2 000 cannon destroyed by the battalion were during this year. Of the 107 tanks used by the unit between November 1942 and the end of April 1945, 85 were destroyed in battle, fifteen or so were scuttled, the rest captured or sent back to the factory.
*(Author's illustration)*

*Above.*
**Tiger 308 seems to have suffered a lot. The crew hasn't bothered to repair the Zimmerit protection and has painted the tank number directly on the steel.** *(BA)*

*Above, right.*
**4th July 1944. Moving in the Dünaburg sector. The battalion still had 52 Tigers.** *(WS)*

*Right.*
**The Tiger 'Hildegard' in June 1944. A red five is scarcely visible, so we have the choice between tank 105, 115, 205, 215, 305 and 315.** *(WS)*

*Left.*
**A mine seems to have done considerable material damage but the crew seems to take this in good spirit.** *(WS)*

*Below.*
A Tiger with a particularly dashing crew, judging by its uniform.
*(WS)*

*Above.*
Photos of the Winter 1944-45 are very rare, as there was a severe shortage of photographic material.
*(WS)*

*Right.*
**Tiger 221, abandoned before Leningrad in the summer of 1943, is towed by a turretless KV 1 through Moscow in 1945. It was placed in the Army Museum, where it still is.**
*(G. Gorokhoff)*

*Above.*
**A Tiger from the Schwer Panzer-Abteilung 503 in January 1943. Under the Winter camouflage the standard grey of German armour can be seen. The figures are white with black outline.** *(BA)*

*Inset*
**s.Pz-Abt. 503's unit sign, very seldom seen.**
*(Author's illustration)*

Created at Neuruppin with personnel from Pz.-Rgt 5 and 6 on the 6th April 1942, it had two companies on the 4th May 1943 and then three in February 1944. It fought in January 1943 in the Don sector near Rostov. The battalion then participated in Operation Zitadelle in the sector of Bielgorod, Chmerinka, in the Kamenez-Podolsk-Tcherkassy inferno and in the Tarnopol sector. Committed on the Normandy front in the summer of 1944, it was then sent to Hungary and on the 21st December 1944, it became the s.Pz.-Abt "Feldherrnhalle" and incorporated in the Panzerkorps of the same name. Its last fight occured to the north of Vienna. The unit's score was impressive with 1 700 Allied tanks and nearly 2 000 cannon destroyed. *Feldwebel* Knispel accounted for 162 enemy tanks, *Oberfähnrich* Rondorf 106 and *Feldwebel* Gärtner more than a hundred. 176 Tiger Is and 76 Tiger IIs were used by the unit.

**Operations zones of s.Pz-Abt. 503**

*Left.*
**Tiger No. 111 during January 1943. The machine has two tool boxes on the front.**
*(WS)*

*Left.*
**Tiger No. 111 during January 1943. The machine has two tool boxes on the front.**
*(WS)*

**A Tiger of the s.Pz.-Abt. 503's 2nd company during the Winter of 1943 (January-February). The absence of a specific Rommelkiste for Tiger tanks lead to improvisation, as here with the use of stowage bins for Panzer IIIs or IVs. The Battalion insignia is on the front, next to the radio operator's station.**
*(Author's illustration)*

*Right.*
**Another view of Tiger 111. In the turret are *Unteroffiziere* Bieder and Mundrey. Note the front left mud-guard which has been torn off with the probable loss of the tool box.**
*(WS)*

*Left.*
**February 1942. Tiger 212 of the 2nd company. The battalion only has two companies and a mixture of Panzer VIs and IIIs. Note the 200 litre fuel drums on the rear of the machine.**
*(WS)*

*Below.*
**Tiger 100 (Stab of the 1st company). As there isn't any snow, white camouflage is not adopted. The machine is painted grey like all the others.**
*(WS)*

*Below.*
**One of the rare photographs showing the battalion insignia, a Tiger's head, on the front plate.**
*(BA)*

*Inset.*
**Color rendition of s. Pz.-Abt. 503.'s unit insignia.**
*(Author's illustration)*

**Tank No. 121. No less than 250 impacts can be counted on this Tiger but the crew - a little groggy - got out unscathed. Tiger 141, which fought alongside, suffered the same fate.**
*(WS)*

*Below.*
**January 1943, Tiger 224, a gift from the 2nd company of the s.Pz.-Abt 502 at Proletarskaja.**
*(WS)*

*Left.*
**Another gift from the 2nd company of the s.Pz.-Abt 502. The new crew has retained the unit insignia on the front plate.**
*(BA)*

*Bottom right.*
**Ten Tigers reinforce the 1st company on 11th April 1943.** *(WS)*

26th June 1943. A manoeuvre is carried out in front of
a Turkish delegation. These were the last exercises
before Operation Zitadelle.
*(WS)*

*Below.*
**Tiger 323 crossing a river during the same exercise.**
*(WS)*

*Right.*
**231 passes another machine from the company.
Note the absence of camouflage.**
*(ECPA)*

A superb view from above of 231 after several days fighting. Zitadelle lasted from 4th to 13th July 1943.
(ECPA)

*Below.*
233 follows the move. The s.Pz.-Abt.503 only lost three Tigers during Operation Zitadelle.
(ECPA)

A Tiger of the s.Pz.-Abt. 503. On the 10th January 1943, this Tiger was so severely hit - more than 250 shots- that it was removed from the front and sent back to a workshop for repairs in Germany. The crew was unhurt. The Rommelkiste came again from a Panzer III. The shape of the figure 1 is characteristic of the unit. Subsequently the shape of the figures varied considerably from one company to another.

*Above.*
**Tiger 21 hidden behind an isba. The ground in the region was very varied and created many problems for the attackers.**
*(ECPA)*

*Right.*
**On the left a destroyed, trackless Grant. The Tiger is showing the number 334.**
*(ECPA)*

*Below.*
**The diversity of the shapes of the numbers is visible between companies and within the companies, between the platoons.**
*(ECPA)*

A pause for a picnic for this crew. The basket made
of wire mesh contains a part of the machine's tools.
(ECPA)

*Above.*
**Tiger 332 in front of 323. The difference between the figures is quite visible.** *(ECPA)*

*Right.*
**Tiger II - I of the Stab and a Tiger of the 3rd company. Note the trailer with fuel barrels behind Tiger II.**
*(ECPA)*

*Below.*
**Several Tigers of the 2nd and 3rd companies have taken up their positions prior to an attack. The shot is taken from a seventh Tiger.** *(ECPA)*

*Opposite page.*
**Note the multiple impacts on the hull front and side of this Tiger. No. 242 has lost its front mud guard.**
*(ECPA)*

*Left.*
**Tiger 242 has received two impacts from the famous anti-tank rifle Degtiarev PTRD. It was insufficient to destroy a tank like the Tiger, but it could damage it.**
*(WS)*

*Right.*
**Another view of Tiger 242. The shell from the PTRD anti-tank rifle penetrates 4.5cm of steel at 100m and 3.5 at 300.**
*(WS)*

A Tiger of the 2nd company of the s.Pz.-Abt. 503. The shape of the figure 2 is typical of the battalion. During May 1942, the Tigers of the 503rd also wore white numbers (1st company) as well as black (2nd and 3rd companies). During Operation Zitadelle, the figures were uniformly painted in black. This machine from the first series - according to the shape of the lateral mud-guard - is a veteran of the fighting of the Winter of 1942-43 and supported the 19th Panzerdivision's efforts in the Kursk salient.
(Author's illustration)

*Left.*
**A very good shot of Tiger 334 with a missing wheel. The movable hooks support the beams used for crossing muddy terrain.**
*(ECPA)*

*Above.*
**Operation *Zitadelle*. This tank commander in fighting gear is probably the captain Burmester.**
*(ECPA)*

46

*Previous page, top.*
**Tiger 333. The last figure is slightly higher than the first two. The photographs are misleading; in reality, the weather is not sunny, it's raining heavily. This can be seen from the muddy ground.**
*(ECPA)*

*Right.*
**Tiger 334 next to a reconnaissance column from the 2nd SS-Pz- Div. "Das Reich". The tank commander is** *Hauptmann* **Scherf.**
*(ECPA)*

*Bottom.*
**Bad weather transformed the ground into a bog. The fighting has been very heavy judging by the marks left on Tiger 332.**
*(ECPA)*

*Right.*
**The same machine seen from another angle. Next to the heavy calibre marks on the armour, traces from an anti-tank rifle can be seen 15 cm from the sighting device opening on the gun mantle.**
*(ECPA)*

*Bottom right.*
**Before towing, you have to be able to attach the towing cables, which seems to be very dirty job, requiring a good sense of balance.**
*(ECPA)*

47

*Top.*
**Tiger 321, whose spare track link rack on the front plate has been torn away. Note the general condition of the machine.**
*(ECPA)*

*Above.*
**A Tiger from the 3rd company of the s.Pz.-Abt. 503, on which can be seen three different types of figures on the turret. Painting the Balkenkreuz on the turret and on the Rommelkiste was a very rare practice. These markings were rather more discreet after the Polish campaign. The unit figure of the 333 is not in line with the others.**
*(Author's illustration)*

*Left.*
**A tank commander conjuring up the picture of a 'U-bootsmann'. Note the use of two different headsets.**
*(ECPA)*

*Right.*
**Another view of a Tiger which is normally misattributed. The 9th company of the Totenkopf was identified by the number 9, not by a 1.**
*(BA)*

*Right.*
**These Tigers are attributed to the 3. SS-Pz.-Div. "Totenkopf" as well. They actually belonged to the 1st company of the s.Pz.- Abt. 503.**
*(BA)*

*Below.*
**Refuelling 334 before going back to the front.**
*(ECPA)*

*Left.*
**Another Tiger from the 1st company during Operation Zitadelle. The camouflage is not typical of the rest of the unit.**
(BA)

*Above.*
**Two Tigers from the 3rd company preparing to attack with a Waffen-SS unit.**
(BA)

*Above.*
**This Tiger is often attributed to the s.Pz.-Abt. 504 in Tunisia. In fact it belonged to the 1st company of the s.Pz.-Abt. 503 during Operation Zitadelle. The white triangles on the SdKfz 9s are typical of the unit.**
(BA)

*Right.*
**A Tiger from the 1st company seems to be waving with its twisted mudguards.**
(BA)

*Above.*
**Tiger 300 of the 3rd company's commander reversing under cover of a smoke screen.**
*(WS)*

*Top right.*
**During the retreat following Operation Zitadelle, the s.Pz.- Abt. 503 lost no tanks. It had lost only three beforehand during fifty days of intense fighting.**
*(WS)*

*Right.*
**On the 30th September, the unit still has 39 Tigers in spite of very heavy fighting.** *(WS)*

*Below.*
**The machines - in this case, those of the 1st company - are readied for the upcoming battles.** *(BA)*

*Bottom right.*
**The Tigers are lined up quietly in a hangar, so that the mechanics can work on them, sheltered from the bad weather.**
*(BA)*

*Right.*
**During January 1944, the Tigers of the 503rd fought alongside the Panthers of the Pz.-Rgt.11 (6 Pz.-Div.) under *Major* Bäke. There were 68 operational Tigers, which was exceptional for such a unit. *Major* Bäke, at the head of his forty-six Panthers, turned out to be an excellent tactician.** *(WS)*

*Below.*
**Tiger 312 with, from left to right, corporal Sautier, and *Unteroffiziere* Matthes and Lange.** *(WS)*

*Below right.*
**January 1944. Tiger 136 (the number is just visible on the rear of the machine). The camouflage is similar to that adopted during the Winter of 1942-43 by the s.Pz.- Abt. 502.** *(DR)*

**A tank cemetery, 30th March 1944. Twenty-one damaged Tigers in this depot fell into the hands of the Soviet troops.** *(KM)*

*Above.*
**A Tiger of the 1st company of the s.Pz.-Abt. 503. The 121 was an old campaigner who had been in combat for fifteen months. It is recognisable by its mudguards, typical of the first series and by the famous Rommelkiste, characteristic of the s.Pz.-Abt. 503. The shape of the cross is also characteristic of the first production models. The 121 fought with the 11. Panzer-Regiment within s.Pz-Rgt "Bäke" until it was lost on 15th March 1944 in the Skalat sector.**
*(Author's illustration)*

53

*Left.*
**Another shot showing
200 and 221. All these
machines were captured
without firing a shot, a
godsend for the Russians.**
*(KM)*

*Below left.*
**A unit detached from the
503rd fought under the
name of Kampfgruppe
Mittermeier in the
Tarnopol sector.**
*(WS)*

*Left.*
**One of the last survivors
of the fighting, in March
1944.**
*(WS)*

*Opposite page*
**122 in front of No. 301 of
the s.Pz.-Abt. 507 in May
1944. It seems that a tow
will be necessary.**
*(ECPA)*

*Right.*
*Hauptmann* Scherf aboard Tiger 122 of the ex-Kampfgruppe Mittermeier. He served with other Tigers, training Hungarian crews. Scherf couldn't imagine then the disaster awaiting him in Normandy.
*(ECPA)*

*Below.*
A Tiger of the 2nd company of the s.Pz.-Abt. 503 during the fighting in the Oratoff region, end of January-February 1944. In five days, the battalion and the Pz -Rgt 11 (using Panthers) destroyed 267 Soviet armour for the loss of three Tigers and four Panthers. At this time, the battalion had 68 Tigers, a number which can be explained by the normal quota (45 tanks) being joined by the two dozen Tigers surviving from the beginning of Winter 1943-44. In a month more than 12 Tigers from Kampfgruppe Bäke were lost. The end came in mid-April for the others. On the 30th March, 24 mainly unserviceable tanks were abandoned to the Red Army, only seven others being able to escape the Soviet offensive. The battalion was made up then sent to the West where a less glorious destiny awaited it...
*(Author's illustration)*

221

*Above.*
**Tiger 114 with its Hungarian driver/mechanic.**
*(ECPA)*

*Above.*
**Driving exercise through ruins in Hungary. The Tigers of Kampfgruppe Mittermeier did not bear any camouflage over the sand yellow.**
*(ECPA)*

*Left.*
**Gunnery training for these Hungarian crews. Note the all-steel wheels.**
*(ECPA)*

In the Spring of 1944, a company from the s.Pz.-Abt 503 was attached to Kampfgruppe Mittermeyer in the Tarnopol area. Subsequently, the tanks were used to train Hungarian soldiers in the Kolomea region. *Hauptmann* Scherf was part of this detachment. In the same series of turret numbers can be included tanks 115, 121,122 and 123. The placing of the numbers varied according to the machines.
*(Author's illustration)*

*Above.*
**1 May 1943, the Tiger No. II of the battalion's Stab in Belgium. The tank is using transport tracks for the railroad trip towards the Eastern front.**
*(DR)*

*Inset.*
**s.Pz-Abt. 505 unit insignia. The original sign (left), and the new sign (right) displayed as of the Spring of 1944.**
*(Author's illustrations)*

Created on the 29th January 1943 at Fallingsbostel with elements of the 3rd and 26th Panzer-Divisions. It took part in the 2nd Panzer Division's engagements in April 1943, to the east of Orel. Then the battalion took part in Operation Zitadelle, in the sectors of Orel, the Dniepr and the north of Ukraine. The first phase of the engagements ended in the Cholm sector. After a rehaul, the 505th was engaged in the sector of Narew,

and then in East Prussia, Goldap, Königsberg and Samland. The last encounters with the Tigers of this unit were at Pillau. The battalion's score was 900 Soviet tanks destroyed, of which 68 went to *Oberleutnant* Knarth, 50 to *Oberleutnant* Mausberg. 78 Tiger Is and 48 Tiger IIs were used by the unit.

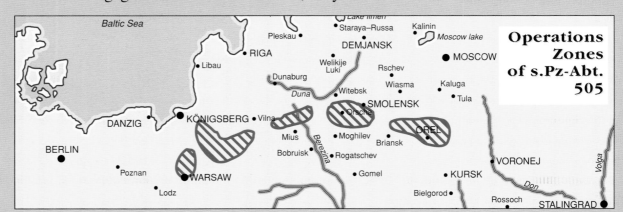

**Operations Zones of s.Pz-Abt. 505**

*Below.*
A Tiger of the 2nd company of the s.Pz.-Abt. 505 during Operation Zitadelle at the beginning of July 1943. The main characteristic is the fact that beams or tree trunks (for crossing gaps, etc.) are placed on the sides of the Tigers. It was an unusual practice, that was however to be found also in the s.Pz.-Abt. 503. The camouflage consists of wide brown stripes on a sand base. In most cases, the battalion insignia is painted on the front left hull, on the driver's side. During Zitadelle, the Tigers of the battalion destroyed more than 60 tanks in the sector of Hill 274.5 for the total loss of five Tigers.
*(Author's illustration)*

*Top.*
The combat tracks, which will be put on after unloading in the Orel sector, are dragged under the hull. *(DR)*

*Left.*
View from the window of a Belgian house. A large number of beams can be seen, serving to support the machine during transportation, even the gun barrel seems to be supported.
*(DR)*

The s. Pz.-Abt. 505
first unit insignia, used
until the beginning
of 1944.
*(Author's illustration)*

*Left.*
**Arrival at Orel in May
1943 of No. II. The
machine is in very good
condition and has not
participated in any
combat yet.**
*(WS)*

*Left.*
**Another shot of the same
tank. At this time, the
unit only had 20 Tigers
and 25 Pz.IIIs. It got its
full AFV complement in
June 1943.**
*(WS)*

*Bottom left.*
**From May to June 1943,
the battalion carried out
exercises with the 2nd
Pz.Div. and the
Funklenk-Kompanie 312
(using the radio
controlled destruction
machine Borgward B IV)
in the Orel-Glazunovka
sector.**
*(KM)*

*Below.*
**The Tiger II during a
preparation exercise for
Operation Zitadelle.**
*(WS)*

Tiger 114 of the 1st company had a particularity: the use of barbed wire protection in case the enemy tried to board the tank. Note the spare track links on the turret, which means a different position for the three identification figures.
*(BA)*

*Above.*
**Another Tiger from the unit wearing the markings of the 1st Company, 4th platoon, 1st vehicle, May 1943.**
*(KM)*

Tiger 214 of the 2nd company presents the same characteristics. The bison insignia is particularly clear.
*(ECPA)*

*Left.*
**Tiger 233 of the same company, June 1943, Glazunovka sector.**
*(KM)*

*Above.*
**A few days before the start of Operation Zitadelle, Tigers 321 and 323 take up their positions. In the background are several SdKfz 251s, one of which is equipped with the Wuhrfrahm 40 rocket launcher.**
*(ECPA)*

*Right.*
**On the 5th July, the s.Pz.-Abt. 505 alone destroyed forty-two T34s, causing the Soviet 15th Infantry Division to collapse. During the fighting on the 1st July, the 1st company lost its commander, *Hauptmann* Riedesel.**
*(WS)*

*Left.*
**Tiger No. II seen from the rear. Note the generalised use of the Feiffel air filters within the unit.**
*(KM)*

**A Tiger of the 2nd company of the s.Pz.-Abt. 505, at the beginning of February 1944, during the fighting in the Toporino sector. Its commander was *Leutnant* Scholz, who took part in the destruction of 46 T 34s in this sector between the 3rd and the 10th February 1944. The machine is particularly interesting as it shows at the same time, the new cupola and the old filters of the early series tanks, something rather unique. The crossing beam can be seen on this machine, and painted white. The turret number 213 is barely legible on the front, and on the Rommelkiste.**
*(Author's illustration)*

*Above.*
**After several days on the line, Tiger No. II seems almost intact in spite of the intensity of the fighting.**
*(WS)*

*Right*
**In the undergrowth a Tiger awaits the next engagement. On the right, the exhaust pipe of a Pz.III, July 1943.**
*(WS)*

Operation Zitadelle gets bogged down in the northern sector of the Heeres Gruppe Mitte. Soviet resistance hardened progressively. (BZS)

*Above and inset, right.*
An impressive quantity of ammunition is required and the lorries and Muni-Panzers are not spared. Note the use of *Schürzen* on some Muni-Pz.III. (ECPA)

*Right.*
*Major* Sauvant in his Tiger of the unit's Stab. (BA)

*Above.*
**This Pz.IV of the 20th Pz.Division (identified by its little elephant on the Rommelkiste) is in bad shape, whereas Tiger 114 seems intact.**
*(ECPA)*

*Right.*
**Tiger 231. Note that the last number of the tanks in the 2nd company was sometimes painted on a sand background, lighter than the base colour used normally.**
*(BA)*

*Above left.*
**The crew of Tiger 133 having a break. On the 7th July, the unit lost three Tigers against an anti-tank barrage. These were the only losses during the whole of Operation Zitadelle for this battalion.** *(WS)*

*Above.*
**Three crew members of the old Tiger No. II.** *(WS)*

*Left.*
**Resupplying a Tiger during the defensive phase of the battle of Kursk. In the foreground, a 4.5 tonne Büssing, and in the background Tiger 223.** *(BZS)*

**Rail transport in the Witebsk sector on the 16th and 17th November 1943. Tank 223 can be recognised in second position.** *(KM)*

*Left.*
**Tiger 123 on 11th December 1943. The clothing is a bit light... that or the Winter issue has not followed.**
*(BA)*

*Bottom.*
**Tank 213 partly hand painted for the Winter.**
*(WS)*

*Below left.*
**The same tank, end of Autumn, beginning of Winter 1943. The machine has been marked by the fighting and the cold is getting worse, judging by the crew's clothing.**
*(WS)*

*Above.*
**A Tiger of the Stabskompanie (Headquarters company) of the s.Pz.-Abt. 505. At the end of the Winter of 1943-44, the Tigers received a new identification system. The numbers were painted on the gun and a charging cavalier painted on the turret side. The Roman numeral III is outlined in white, which doesn't show up very well on the whitewash background. The yellow band on the gun, for platoon commanders's tanks, apparently only appeared later. This Tiger took part in the last operations of the Winter, being replaced by another tank with the new commander's cupola.**
*(Author's illustration)*

**Winter 1943-44, the first Winter for the unit. The tanks have been painted white. Note the shape of the bar that is holding the spare links.**
*(WS)*

*Below left.*
**A curious shot of one of the 505th's Tigers, showing a crewman or a Russian's or German's dead body. The boots are Russian; the position of the legs is set and seems unnatural.**
*(WS)*

*Below.*
**Early 1944 in the immense Russian plain, Tiger 505 stops next to the battalion commander's car, during a pause.**
*(BA)*

**The fighting's intensity has not diminished. This shot was taken through the observation port of another tank.** *(BA)*

**No. 211, seen from the same tank, has taken up the ideal position for its shot.**
*(BA)*

Above.
**Our old No. II still serving. A ladder is used for climbing aboard, to avoid slipping on the frozen metal.**
(WS)

Left and center.
**Dirty work for the crews: a repaired track has to be fitted back on a Tiger from the 2nd company. The track is laid out flat for the Tiger to drive onto; all the men set to.**
(BA)

*Left.*
**In trying to pass round a bridge, Tiger 231 has got stuck. It will not get out under its own steam.** *(BA)*

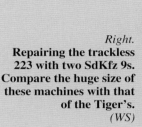

*Right.*
**Repairing the trackless 223 with two SdKfz 9s. Compare the huge size of these machines with that of the Tiger's.** *(WS)*

*Right.*
**The manoeuvre has succeeded, and the Tiger is out of the rut. Even though it is a tank with a new commander's cupola, it still has the Feiffel filters.** *(BA)*

*Below.*
**The helping Tiger is in position for the next operation.** *(BA)*

*Bottom right.*
**Tank 200 already in a defensive position. The machine was painted white, now very much washed out.** *(WS)*

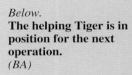

*Right.*
**At the end of the Winter 1944 appears a new insignia for the unit: a knight. This machine is a Kursk veteran, judging by the tank commander's cupola. There's no Zimmerit apparently.**
*(WS)*

**A Tiger of the 3rd company of the s.Pz.-Abt. 505 in the region of Nowe Koszary. The tanks of the battalion have kept tree trunks and beams attached to their sides. From Autumn 1943, the numbers were painted on the gun, first without a colour background (Winter 1943-44), then, because of problems of identification, on a yellow background in the spring of 1944. The cavalier's colour actually varied according to the availability of paint.**
*(Author's illustration)*

**Detail of the knight insignia chosen by the battalion during the Spring of 1944. The colors are improvised and do NOT follow the colour code for companies:** *Stab* **(white), 1st Coy (red), 2nd Coy (yellow), 3rd Coy (green).**
*(Author's illustrations)*

*Right.*
**133 in the foreground and a veteran in the background. The unit only had 20 Tigers left at the end of the Winter of 1944.**
*(WS)*

*Above.*
**In March 1944, the Tigers were overhauled in the Orscha sector. There were twenty three in the battalion. Despite the fighting, there were no losses between 22nd February and 27th June 1944.**
*(BA)*

*Above right.*
**A well-known view of No. 300 with *Kletterbalken* (crossing beams) on its sides. Lt. Röder in the turret.**
*(BA)*

*Right.*
**Another Tiger on the same day at the beginning of July. The battalion destroyed 128 Soviet tanks in two week's fighting.**
*(BA)*

*Previous page, top left.*
**Spring 1944. A new Tiger delivered in September 1943 replaced old No. II, lost in the turmoil. It is possible that this new number was attributed at the end of the Winter 1944.**
*(WS)*

*Previous page, top right.*
**Repairing the the right sprocket wheel. The knight insignia can just be made out on the turret.**
*(WS)*

*Right.*
**Lt. Röder with his gunner in the foreground, in the Augustowo sector.**
*(BA)*

*Below.*
**Tank No. 300. Total losses for the unit in the East were 21 tanks.**
*(BA)*

*Above.*
**Scarcely recognisable on the second Tiger is part of the typical yellow W unit sign on the rear of the turret, indicating the 3rd company, November 1943.**
*(BA)*

*Right.*
**Unit signs of s.Pz-Abt. 506.**
*(Author's illustrations)*

Formed on the 20th July 1943 from the IIIrd battalion of the 33rd Pz.-Rgt. of the 9th Pz.-Div. at St Pölten. It was immediately committed in September 1943 at the Saporoje Bridgehead with the Ferdinand Jagdtigers of the 653rd s.Pz.-Jäger Abt., then in the sector of Oratow; it crossed the Dniestr in the region of Stanislaw in April 1944.

In August it handed over its Tigers to the s.Pz.-Abt.507. In Sep-

tember 1944, it was refurbished and trained on the new Tiger IIs. From October 1944, it was engaged in the West (a company fought at Arnhem) in the sectors of Aachen, in the Eifel, at Bastogne, Siegen and finally the Ruhr. The unit was disbanded at Iserlohn. It had a score of 400, mostly on the Eastern front, and one hundred in the West. 94 Tiger Is and 74 Tiger IIs were used by the battalion.

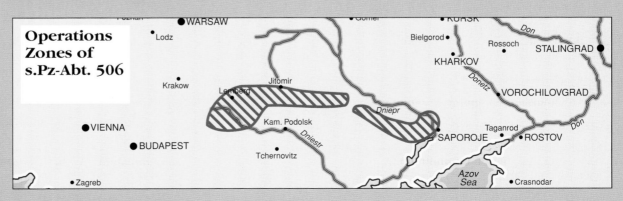

**Operations Zones of s.Pz-Abt. 506**

*Left.*
**The Tigers, here those of the 3rd company, arrive on the Eastern front by rail transport.**
*(WS)*

*Bottom left.*
**The Tiger having hit its target and still keeping it covered, moves carefully past it; infantrymen start to get up and move on.**
*(WS)*

*Bottom right.*
**A casualty is loaded onto white No. 5 from the 1st company.**
*(WS)*

**A Tiger from the 1st Coy./s.Pz.-Abt. 506 during the fighting in September 1943 near Lukanjowka. The fighting was very heavy in this sector and the Tigers rarely got the upper hand. On the 1st January 1944, Abt. 506 lost 19 Tigers, of which one was destroyed by a German PaK gun. White was the colour of the 1st company. The figures and the insignia were the same colour, except for the blazon (red) and the unit insignia (yellow and black).**
*(Author's illustration)*

*Left.*
**Infantry on the rear of Tiger red No. 6. The men are happy to be able to warm their feet up a bit on the engine covers.**
*(WS)*

*Below.*
**A good view of the unit's insignia. The white of the W identifies the 1st company.**
*(WS)*

**s.Pz-Abt. 506's unit signs :**
– green: Stab
– white: 1. Kompanie
– red : 2. Kompanie
– yellow: 3. Kompanie.
*(Author's illustrations)*

*Left.*
**A column of Tigers in the Lemberg sector, during the Winter of 1943-44.**
*(WS)*

*Opposite page.*
**Early March 1944, the 1st company reaches the town of Lemberg.**
*(WS)*

*Opposite page, far right.*
**The machines have been painted white over the Zimmerit. A bit of number red 5 is just visible.**
*(WS)*

*Right.*
**Three Tigers from the 1st and 3rd companies ford a river during the Winter of 1943-44.**
*(WS)*

*Right.*
**Three Tigers from the 1st and 3rd companies ford a river during the Winter of 1943-44.**
*(WS)*

*Below.*
**A Tiger of the 3rd company of the s.Pz.-Abt. 506 at the beginning of 1944 in the Oratow sector. Since September 1943, the battalion had destroyed more than 200 Soviet tanks, but had only ten working tanks at the end of January 1944. The last week of January**

**saw the loss of 16 Tigers confronted with the excellent anti-tank defences of the Red Army in the north - eastern sector of Zybrettw and in the Wladislawtschik and Nowelskii regions. Note the use of Zimmerit.**
*(Author's illustration)*

**Spring 1944. The unit received forty-five new Tigers.** *(BA)*

**Summer 1944, in the sector of Sisbodha. Tank 13 of the 3rd company in a defensive position.** *(WS)*

Tiger 13 of the 1st company passes through a recaptured village.
(WS)

*Below.*
A Tiger of the 2nd company of the s.Pz.-Abt. 506, the second vehicle of the 3rd platoon. At the end of March 1944, the battalion received the new Tigers with all-steel road wheels. Out of the 45 tanks of the quota, twenty-odd were operational. The battalion fought on to the end of July 1944 with this type of tank; then it received the new Tiger IIs. The surviving Tiger Is, about ten of them, were handed over to the s.Pz.-Abt. 503. The remainder, about thirty, had been lost in a single day on the 22nd July during the retreat in the Stepance-Ladance sector. The day before, a Tiger destroyed a JS1 with a single shot at a range of 3.9kms (2.5miles).
*(Author's illustration)*

*Below.*
**Summer 1944. The 3rd company C.O., *Oberleutnant* Hoffmann, poses in front of his Tiger with his crew. Soon the unit was to be equipped with the new Tiger II.**
*(WS)*

*Bottom right.*
**Another fording operation, with Tiger red 2 in the foreground and in the background, No. 13 of the 1st company.** *(WS)*

*Above.*
**This shot shows tank A of the unit commander in the Tarnopol sector, in April 1944.**
*(BA)*

*Right.*
**Unit sign of s.Pz-Abt. 507.**
*(Author's illustration)*

Formed in September 1943 in Vienna with the elements from the 1st Abt. of the Pz.-Rgt. 3 and from the 1st Abt. of the Pz.-Rgt. 4. A part of the battalion (from Pz.-Rgt. 3) received Panthers and rejoined its original unit. The remainder left Vienna for training in the Autumn of 1943 in the sector of Le Mans (France), then at Wezep in the Zwolle region in Holland. At the end of March 1944, the battalion was engaged in the sectors of Tarnopol-Brody, then Baranowitschi, and Slonim-Ostrolenka. The retreat brought it to Warsaw, then to the south of Danzig. In March 1945, the unit was equipped with Tiger IIs. In one year the battalion destroyed 600 enemy tanks while it used 80 Tiger Is altogether.

**Operations Zones of s.Pz-Abt. 507**

# Abteilung 507

*Left.*
**Although badly touched up, this photograph shows perfectly well the shape of the figures on No. 100 (1st company).**
*(IWM)*

*Below.*
**The machines were continually repaired. A mechanic is doing some welding on this one.**
*(WS)*

*Above.*
**A Tiger of the 1st company of the s.Pz.-Abt. 507, in April 1944. The battalion was formed late and was committed in March 1944. It was however rated amongst the best of the Tiger units of the Heer. In eleven months' fighting on the Eastern front, the battalion destroyed more than 500 tanks. At this period, the Tiger was beginning to encounter sterner adversaries than in 1942-43. The most formidable were the JS 2s, T 34/85s, SU 100s and SU152s whose cannon and armour were the same if not better than the heavy German tank's.**
*(Author's illustration)*

*Above.*
**A concentration of armour in the Tarnopol sector. A Hummel, a Tiger and a Stu III can be seen. Note the numerous shell-holes in the background.**
*(BA)*

*Above.*
**The unit commander attacks. The smoke canisters were used to hide the tanks from the enemy.**
*(BA)*

*Right.*
**Panzergrenadiers support the assault aboard a SdKfz 251 personnel carrier. Note the wide track prints left by the Tigers.**
*(BA)*

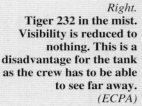

*Right.*
**Tiger 232 in the mist. Visibility is reduced to nothing. This is a disadvantage for the tank as the crew has to be able to see far away.**
*(ECPA)*

*Inset*
**The s.Pz-Abt. 507 unit sign.**
*(Author's illustration)*

*Below.*
**Tiger 114 in the region of Zichenau; in the background No. 313.**
*(BA)*

*Above.*
**This Tiger of the s.Pz.-Abt. 507 belongs to the 2nd company commander, *Oblt* Max Wirsching, who took command of the battalion for three days from the 17 to the 19th January 1945, replacing the wounded *Hauptmann* Fritz Schöck. In three days the battalion destroyed 136 Russian tanks without loss. In spite of the superiority of the JS 2, the Tiger had a better firing rate. The JS2's gun used two part ammunition: shell and cartridge, a fatal disadvantage when faced with the Tiger's 88 mm. On the 14th January 1945, the 3rd company destroyed 22 JS 2s at point blank range.**
*(Author's illustration)*

83

*Previous page, top left.*
**After fighting in September 1944 alongside the 6th Panzerdivision, the machines are showing signs of wear and tear.** *(WS)*

*Previous page, top right.*
**The track links placed on the hull front are not typical of Abteilung 507, as other units did this.** *(BZS)*

*Previous page, bottom.*
**The 1st company's commander tank with the left-hand side running gear destroyed by a mine. Summer 1944.** *(ECPA)*

*Right.*
**Resupplying Tiger ...14** *(BZS)*

*Below.*
**This Tiger has been scuttled by its crew in January 1945. Soon afterwards, the unit was re-equipped with Tiger IIs.** *(WS)*

*Below.*
**A Tiger of the 3rd company of the s.Pz.-Abt. 507, in the region of Zambrow in August 1944. Its commander was Klaus-Peter Müller, who saved the crew of 331 (*Ofw.* Klaus Diez) on 25th August in the fighting to the north-west of Sniadowo. Note the placing of the spare track links on the turret, which in principle gave more protection against large caliber shells. This type of arrangement and the shape of the figures enable the unit to be identified for certain. The join between the numbers and the links on the turret are not very precise.**
*(Author's illustration)*

*Above.*
**Tiger 233 in the region of Kichnew during the Winter of 1943-44.**
*(WS)*

*Right.*
**Unit sign of s.Pz-Abt. 509.**
*(Author's illustration)*

Formed in September 1943 at Schwetzingen using the Pz.-Rgts. 202 and 204 as a base. It trained at Sennelager, then at Mailly-le-Camp (France). At the end of October, beginning of November, the 509th was committed in the south of Russia in the sector of Fastowetz, Jitomir, Sasslaw, then Kamenez-Podolsk. After a period of restructuring, the battalion fought in Hungary at the beginning of January 1945 in the Stuhlweissenburg area. In March it fought in the same sector alongside the First Panzer-Division. The rest of the unit surrendered, after a long retreat along the Moldau, to American troops at Kaplitz. The battalion destroyed 500 Soviet tanks and used 70 Tiger Is and 50 Tiger IIs. One of its aces was *Ober-feldwebel* Litzke with a score of 76.

**Operations zones of s.Pz-Abt. 509**

SMOLENSK
DANZIG
KÖNIGSBERG • Vilna
Orscha
BERLIN
Mius
Moghilev
Brjansk
OREL
Bobruisk
Rogatschev
VORONEJ
Poznan
Gomel
KURSK
WARSAW
Lodz
Bielgorod
Rossoch
STALINGRAD
Krakow
Jitomir
KHARKOV
Lemberg
VOROCHILOVGRAD
Dniepr
VIENNA
Kam. Podolsk
Taganrod
BUDAPEST
Tchernovitz
SAPOROJE
ROSTOV

# Abteilung 509

*Left.*
**23rd September 1943 at Sennelager, loading the trains for Mailly-le-Camp. The machines are marked with chalked numbers for the operation.**
*(WS)*

*Below.*
**A Tiger of the 509th battalion in France during the training period at Mailly-le-Camp, end of September, beginning of October 1943.**
*(WS)*

*Above.*
**The s.Pz.-Abt. 509 used in part Tigers coming from s.Pz.-Abt. 503 from Summer 1944 onwards, particularly tanks with all-steel road wheels. This one is an older machine, coming probably from s.Pz.-Abt. 501. The Feiffel filters had been removed just before the Winter of 1943-44. The Russian-style script for the numbers was abandoned in the summer of 1944. The machine belonged to the 2nd company.**
*(Author's illustration)*

*Above left.*
**Lieutenant Baker and his crew. The machines seem to be too new to have been to the front.**
*(WS)*

*Above*
**Tiger 23. (last digit unknown). Note the unique Soviet-style shape of the figures in this unit.**
*(WS)*

*Above.*
**Almost two whole crews are sitting astride this Tiger's gun barrel.**
*(WS)*

*Right.*
**Tiger 113 in the region of Jitomir, early 1944.**
*(WS)*

*The machine has still got a bit of camouflage left on the hull side.*
*(WS)*

*Below.*
**Unit sign of Abteilung 509.**
*(Author's illustration)*

*Bottom.*
**July 1944, Tigers being transported by train in the Stanislau sector.**
*(WS)*

*Above.*
**A Tiger of the 2nd company of the s.Pz.-Abt. 509 during the Winter 1943-44. The 212 was the tank of *Unteroffizier* Bellof, who particularly distinguished himself. Note the Feiffel filters. Only the s.Pz.-Abt. 505 and 509 have this equipment at this time and until Spring 1944. The combination of the new cupola and the Feiffel was characteristic of these two battalions. Most of the numbers of these tanks were repainted in black on a white background. The tanks recovered their original colour scheme in the Spring.**
*(Author's illustration)*

89

*Right.*
**This machine is often attributed to the s.SS-Pz.- Abt 502 in Normandy. However, the camouflage scheme does not match that used by that unit.**
*(BA)*

*Below.*
**A Tiger of the 2nd company of the s.Pz.-Abt. 509 in June 1944. After the battle of Buczacz on 20th April 1944 where 18 Tigers held off a Soviet attack, the battalion received 28 new tanks. Some of them sported a slightly unorthodox Zimmerit pattern. The shape of the turret numbers has changed for something more traditional. At the beginning of June 1944, the battalion had 52 Tigers. No. 214 was destroyed on 16 August 1944 by a JS 2.**
*(Author's illustration)*

# 8 - The Schwer Panzer

*Above.*
**Tiger 233 the 8th December 1944 on the Courland front.**
*(BZS)*

*Right.*
**The insignia of s.Pz-Abt. 510.**
*(Author's illustration)*

Formed on the 10th June 1944 at Paderborn with elements from the Panzer-Lehr-Kompanie stationed in Versailles (France) and other units such as Ausbildung.-Abt 500 (a replacement battalion). Training took place at Paderborn and the unit was first committed in July 1944 to the south of Kowno, then in the Vilna sec-

tor, in East Prussia, in the Goldap-Nemmersdorf-Gumbinnen area and in Courland. After a brief overhaul, the unit surrendered to the Allies in the sector of Putlos. The unit had 200 tanks to its credit and used 57 Tiger Is and 6 Tiger IIs.

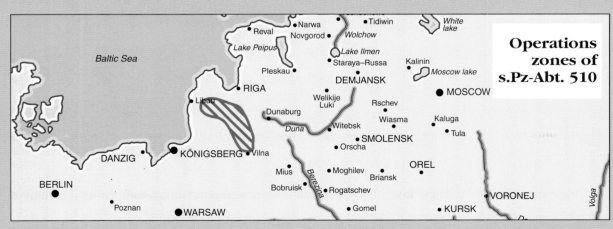

**Operations zones of s.Pz-Abt. 510**

# Abteilung 510

*Right.*
**The battalion insignia, painted on the rear of the hull.**
*(Author's illustration)*

*Left.*
**End of August 1944, between Kelme and Kursenas (Lithuania), on the Courland front. Lt Ehrhard Schulze (in the turret) with his crew:** *Gefreiter* **Krause (driver),** *Obergefreiter* **Otto (radio),** *Obergefreiter* **Dittwald (loader) and** *Unteroffizier* **Jentzsch (gunner).** *(WS)*

*Below.*
**Tiger 132 in rather a bad position. The bridge could not take the weight.**
*(WS)*

*Above.*
**Formed up very late in the conflict, the s.Pz.-Abt.510 was committed at the end of July 1944 in the Wosilickes sector. In mid-August, the battalion was attached to the 7th Panzerdivision. The main characteristic of the unit was to place the number of the tank on the side towards the rear of the turret, a unique feature for a Tiger unit. The shape of the number 3 is similar to that used by the s.Pz.-Abt.501 and 507. The battalion only had Tigers with the all-steel road wheels during its existence. The position of the Balkenkreuz varied from tank to tank.**
*(Author's illustration)*

*Above.*
**This shot reportedly shows
W. Fey's tank on the 8th August
1944 in Normandy, on the Route
Nationale 158. Mr Fey claims to
remember the piece of steel
attached to the front of his machine
perfectly well.**
*(DR)*

*Above right.*
**The same photo coming from other
archives, of better quality, showing
the same scene without the piece of
steel or scratches on the negative.
The date is correct and the unit is
not the s.SS-Pz.-Abt 502, whose
camouflage pattern does not show
here. What is more, the bar which
holds the spare track links does not
tally with any unit known to have
been engaged in Normandy. At any
rate, the s.SS-Pz.-Abt. 502 didn't
even use these bars. This is actually
a Tiger from the 510th battalion, in
July 1944, on the Eastern Front.**
*(BZS)*

*Right.*
**The same scene a few moments
later. W. Fey is not recognisable in
the turret either.**
*(BZS)*

*Above.*
**A Tiger of the 2nd company
carrying parachutists from
the 21st Luftland Div.**
*(DR)*

*Below.*
**The End. The last Tiger
engagements of the unit
were in the Courland
sector. The survivors
surrendered to English
troops.**
*(WS)*

*Above.*
**A tank in the 2nd company
of the s.Pz.-Abt.510 during
the Winter of 1943-44. A
this time, only twenty-odd
Tigers from the battalion
were operational. The 3rd
company which had no
tanks was reformed. In the
course of a counter-attack
on 25th January 1945, the
1st and 2nd companies took
part in the annihilation of
63 Russian tanks, who were
mainly the victims of the 22
Tigers engaged. There were
no Tiger losses. On 10th
April 1945, 13 tanks were
still operational. The 3rd
company was meanwhile
fighting in Germany. It had
six Tiger IIs since the end of
March 1944.**
*(Author's illustration)*

*Inset.*
**The insignia
of Abteilung 510.**
*(Author's illustration)*

95

# 9 - The 4th, then 13th s.SS Pz-Kom

Activated on the 15 August 1942, the unit only received its Tigers at the beginning of 1943. After a brief training period, it took part in operations to recapture Kharkov and established contact with the "Grossdeutschland" Division on the 22nd March 1943. It lost two Tigers out of nine during this period. For Zitadelle it had 14 Tigers. Kursk was the apogee of this unit which literally ravaged the ranks of Soviet armour, for the loss of only two Tigers on the 6th and the 12th July 1943. The unit handed over its remaining Tigers to the 5th Kompanie of the "Das Reich" Division and to the 9th Panzer-Kompanie "Totenkopf". The crews were sent to Italy for retraining.

In November 1943, the fighting took up again in the sector of Kirowograd and was particularly trying. At the end of February 1944, there were only two Tigers left out of 27 committed. Having meanwhile become the s.Pz.-Abt. 101 (501), the unit was engaged in Normandy, then re-equipped with Tiger IIs. Forty-odd Tigers were used in the East during twelve months' fighting, and 400 enemy tanks destroyed. The top-scorers were of course Michaël Wittmann, but also *Obersturmführer* Wendorff with 58 tanks to his credit up to 12th February 1944, and *Rottenführer* Warmbrunn (51 up to 16th April 1944).

*Above.*
**411 with its new camouflage during training.**
*(BA)*

*Left.*
**Formation sign of the 1. SS-Panzerdivision.**
*(Author's illustrationr)*

*Opposite.*
**This Tiger, inspected by Guderian himself, has received a shot directly on the front panel, which explains the extra plate. The photograph was taken after Kursk.**
*(BA)*

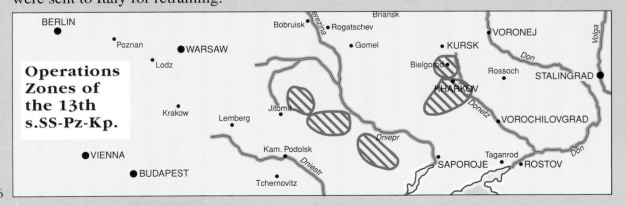

**Operations Zones of the 13th s.SS-Pz-Kp.**

BERLIN · Poznan · WARSAW · Lodz · Krakow · Lemberg · Jitomir · Kam. Podolsk · VIENNA · BUDAPEST · Tchernovitz · Bobruisk · Rogatschev · Gomel · Briansk · KURSK · Bielgorod · KHARKOV · Dniepr · Rossoch · STALINGRAD · VOROCHILOVGRAD · Taganrod · SAPOROJE · ROSTOV · VORONEJ · Don · Volga · Berezina · Donetz · Dniestr

*Left.*
**There are few photographs of the fight for Kharkov. The SS divisions "Das Reich" and "Totenkopf", seem to have been photographed more than the others.**
*(BA)*

*Below.*
**A Tiger of the s.SS.Pz.-Kp. of the 1.SS.Panzergrenadier-Division "Leibstandarte Adolf Hitler" during the fighting for Kharkov. The tank is that of** *Oscha.* **Heinz Mengele. At this period, the Tiger crews had much on their hands with the T 34s, the cold, the snow and the new Tiger's teething troubles. Breakdowns and fires were frequent and unserviceable machines were scuttled. But the main cause of the losses was the accuracy of the Russian anti-tank guns. At this time, M. Wittmann was the tank commander of a Panzer III of the company.**
*(Author's illustration)*

*Above.*
**Three aces from the company. From left to right:**
*Ustuf.* **Wendorf,** *Ostuf.* **Schütte and**
*Ustuf.* **Wittmann.**
*(WS)*

*Above.*
***Obersturmführer* Schütz**
**in Tiger 411.**
*(BA)*

*Right.*
**Three-quarter rear view**
**of Tiger 411.**
*(BA)*

*Right.*
**Panzer-grenadiers perched on the rear of 1332 during Operation Zitadelle.**
*(WS)*

*Below.*
**A Tiger of the s.SS.Pz.-Kp. of the 1. SS-Panzergrenadier-Division "Leibstandarte Adolf Hitler" in April 1943. The 435 was the tank of *Ustuf.* Wendorff. After the fighting in February and March 1943, the machines traded their white camouflage for a sand ochre base with brown stripes. After intensive training, the LAH Tigers were thrown into the Battle of Kursk. Meanwhile the numbers of the tanks were modified. Under the new camouflage can be seen the original grey colour. This Tiger was one of the first series, with staggered side mud-guards.**
*(Author's illustration)*

**Formation sign of the
1. SS-Panzer-Division.**
*(Author's illustration)*

*Left.*
**1311 at the same scene during Zitadelle. Note the
absence of protection for the exhaust pipe.**
*(WS)*

*Below.*
**1334 of *Uscha.* Brandt. The machine has received
numerous impacts. The locally-made mudguards are
slightly curved.**
*(WS)*

*Below.*
**A Tiger of the s.SS.Pz.-Kp. of the 1.SS-Panzergrenadier-Division "Leibstandarte Adolf Hitler" during the Battle of Kursk. The 1325 was the machine of *Uscha.* Franz Standegger. During the two weeks of the battle, the division destroyed 487 Soviet tanks and 204 anti-tank guns. The majority (151 tanks and 87 guns) can be attributed to the Tigers, which were the spearhead of the Division. Soviet propaganda claimed that 700 Tigers were destroyed, five times more than the real number engaged in the fighting... Certain Anglo-american historians, e.g. Alan Bullock, put forward the figure of 17 Tiger Divisions at Kursk, i.e. 2 000 tanks.**

*Above.*
**This Tiger from the 13th company is passing through a burning village. The civilian population was not spared by either side during Operation Zitadelle.**
*(BZS)*

*Below.*
**The shells are piled up on this Tiger, which will be returning to the front line shortly.**
*(KM)*

**The figure for Tiger losses of all Tiger units which participated in the battle (s.Pz.-Abt. 503 and 505 and the heavy companies of the 1st, 2nd and 3rd SS. Panzergrenadier-Divisions and of the Grossdeutschland Division) did not exceed twenty or so.**
*(Author's illustration)*

*Left.*
***Uscha.* Hans Höld's Tiger S12** having its engine
changed at the end of Autumn 1943.
*(BZS)*

*Below.*
***Oscha.* Willy Sadzio's Tiger S45** being overhauled.
*(DR)*

*Below.*
The unit received new Tigers and revelled in the
softness of the Italian climate. This is the S04
of *Oscha.* Kröhn.
*(DR)*

*Right.*
**S45 in difficulty, the freezing mud would often block the road wheels.**
*(DR)*

*Below.*
**The insignia of the 1. SS-Panzer-Division at Kharkov.**
*(Author's illustration)*

*Below.*
**The last operations of the unit in March 1944.**
*(BA)*

Winter of 1943-44. The S45 was the tank of *Uscha.* Herbert Stief. It has been painted white and two track links on the turret are missing, showing the base colour. As on all the Tigers of the company, the unit sign is painted on the left (moving forwards) on a level with the driver's vision slot. At the beginning of April 1944, there was only one Tiger left in the company, that of *Rottenführer* Warmbrunn. The unit was sent to Italy to be reformed, before rejoining the Normandy front.
*(Author's illustration)*

103

The company was created in mid-November 1942 at Fallingsbostel and committed at the beginning of February for the Kharkov offensive. It only had 9 Tigers and lost two during this operation, which led it to the west of Bielgorod. During Zitadelle, it destroyed a lot of armour, only losing one tank. At the end of July, it received ten Tigers from the 13th s.SS Pz.-Kp. "Leibstandarte Adolf Hitler" and fought alongside the SS Division "Totenkopf" in August, in the Mius sector, breaking the Soviet attacks.

Subsequently, it took part in all the rearguard actions in the sectors of Jitomir (November 1943) and Cheptouka (beginning of 1944). Its last three Tigers were scuttled in the sector of Sinkove-Strichkovze.

The company was engaged afterwards as the s.Pz.-Abt 102 (502) in Normandy, then again in the East, equipped with Tiger IIs.

In thirteen months of campaigning, from February 1943 to March 1944, it used and lost thirty-odd Tigers including those given to it by the 13th s.SS Pz.-Kp. "Leibstandarte Adolf Hitler". Among its aces were *Obersturmführer* Kalls who was later taken prisoner in Normandy.

**Operations zones of the s. SS-Pz.-Kp. "Das Reich"**

# S Pz-Kp. "Das Reich"

**Above.**
The same machine from another angle; the tanks are about to be employed immediately.
*(ECPA)*

**Below.**
No. 832, end of February, during an overhaul.
*(ECPA)*

**Above.**
A Tiger from the (8th) heavy company of the 2.SS-Panzergrenadier-Division "Das Reich" during the Winter of 1942-43. The 801 is the machine of *Hstuf.* Herzing. The crew was : *Rottenführer* Blasing (driver), *Oberschütze* Haselbock (radio operator), *Sturmmann* Hinrischen (gunner) and ....Grupe (loader). During a demonstration, the tank broke the ice on which it was moving. It was completely flooded and had to be sent back from the front to be repaired. It rejoined the unit only in August 1943. Meanwhile the crew received Tiger 802, rebaptised 801. In turn the crew of 802 had to wait until August 1943 before getting another tank.

*Above.*
**The protection fairings have been removed from the exhaust pipes, as well as the pipes. The machine has already served two weeks.**
(ECPA)

*Right.*
**Contrasting shades of grey are apparent on the worn parts of the turret.**
(ECPA)

*Below.*
**No. 812 provides support fire in front of the Pz.IIIs of the Division.**
(BA)

*Above left.*
**No. 812 on the way to Bielgorod.**
*(BA)*

*Above.*
**The same scene as on previous page giving a general view of the situation. The tanks are protected by a drop in the ground level.**
*(BA)*

*Left.*
**Two big SdKfz 9s towing broken-down Tiger 822. Technical problems were frequent when the Tigers started to be used.**
*(BA)*

*Below.*
**Mid-March 1943. The offensive reaches its final phase, with Bielgorod as its objective.**
*(WS)*

*Right.*
**The honours after the hard fighting and the rather ephemeral victory.**
*(BA)*

*Left.*
**Himmler in person visits the unit in May 1943. Note the number 823 covering 832.** *(BA)*

*Above.*
**The same machine presenting the details from behind.** *(BA)*

*Below, left.*
**The cross painted on the hull seems enormous and brings to mind that of the s.Pz.-Abt. 502, except for its positioning.** *(BA)*

*Below.*
**This period is rich in ceremonies. Here it's the 20th April 1943, the Führer's birthday, with the tank "Tiki". In the forefront, *Gruppenführer* Krüger.** *(BA)*

*Right.*
**The machine shows an oversize unit insignia on the hull front. Himmler is still in the turret.**
*(BA)*

*Above.*
**Variation of the 2. SS-Panzer-Div. insignia.**
*(Author's illustration)*

*Bottom, right.*
**The same 'Tiki' during training.** *(WS)*

A Tiger of the heavy company of the 2.SS-Panzergrenadier-Division "Das Reich" during a transition period at the beginning of Spring 1943. A camouflage pattern has been improvised with sand yellow and the former number (832) has been turned into 823. The crews underwent intensive training with a view to Operation Zitadelle, and this training was well worth it considering the number of Soviet tanks that were destroyed. But the numerical superiority and the quality of the opponent proved overwhelming even for the Tigers. *(Author's illustration)*

*Left.*
**A field exercise takes place on the same day. This unfortunate Russian village was chosen as the site.**
*(ECPA)*

*Right and below.*
**These two aerial shots show the Tiger in an unusual way: it seems to be a toy.**
*(ECPA)*

*Below.*
**During Operation Zitadelle, Tiger 533 meets a SiG 33 of the 23rd Pz.-Div.**
*(BA)*

*Left.*
**On the plain in the Bielgorod sector. The Tigers are part of the II. SS-Panzergruppe.**
*(BA)*

*Below.*
**The Tigers and some of the 18 T34s serving in the Pz.-Jäger Kompanie of the "Das Reich" Division.**
*(BA)*

*Below.*
**Some Tigers wear a personal sign as well as the divisional sign and the imp.**
*(BA)*

*Right.*
**Variation of the 2. SS-Panzer-Div. unit marking.**
*(Author's illustration)*

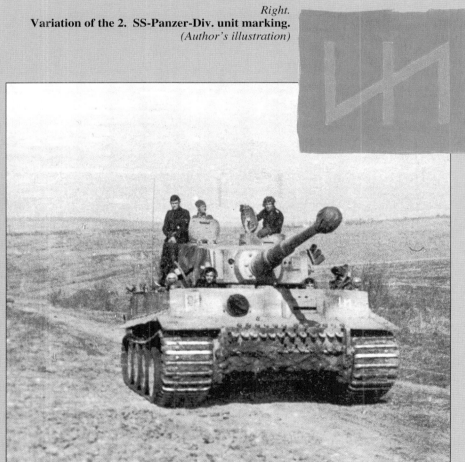

*Right.*
**Hidden behind Tiger S 24, the grenadiers cautiously follow the tanks.**
*(BA)*

*Below.*
**The Tiger has destroyed its target. One can get a better idea of the type of fighting during the Battle of Kursk thanks to such photographs.**
*(BA)*

*Below right.*
**The S24, badly shot up but victorious.**
*(BA)*

A Tiger of the s.SS-Pz.-Kp. of the 2.SS-Panzergrenadier-Division "Das Reich". The machine is camouflaged with sand-coloured paint applied with a brush by the crew on the grey base. *Tiki* was a diminutive of Tiger. The company often used personal insignia. Three victory rings have been painted on the end of the gun barrel, black not being a very widespread colour at the time.
*(Author's illustration)*

*Top left.*
**Fourteen victories for this Tiger, whose gun barrel is being cleaned.**
*(BA)*

*Top right.*
**The division's insignia at that time can be seen on the rear mudguard.**
*(BA)*

*Right.*
**On 1st November 1943, *Oscha.* Soretz receives an award as he has just destroyed the 2 000th tank for the "Das Reich" division. Note the personal insignia behind: a Chinese seal from an ancient ring.**
*(BA)*

113

*Above.*
**End of 1943, fighting in the Jitomir sector: the 533 and the 513 are behind.**
*(BA)*

*Above, right.*
**The photographs in this series were taken in a wood near the the town of Berditchev.** *(BA)*

*Left.*
**Note the two impacts from anti-tank rifles on the front plate, as well as the unit insignia.**
*(BA)*

**Unit marking of the 2. SS-Panzer-Div. from Citadelle until the Winter of 1943-44.**
*(Author's illustration)*

*Right.*
**The little imp and the impacts visible on this other shot of S 33.**
*(BA)*

*Bottom*
**The battered S 13 and S 33 not faring better. The last Tigers of the company were lost in December 1943.**
*(BA)*

*Left.*
A Tiger of the heavy company of the 2.SS-Panzergrenadier-Division "Das Reich" during Operation Zitadelle, beginning of July 1943. At this time, the company was the only Waffen-SS unit to use the initial S of the adjective *Schwer* (heavy) on the turret. The imp cocking his snoot was the emblem of a Kharkov transport company and the stencil was used as it was by the unit after Kharkov. The divisional sign was painted at the front and rear of the hull, but the placing varied. It can be seen thus at the rear under the cross or on the rear left hand mud-guard.
The side hull cross was found on three main places, towards the front as here, halfway along, or between the two as on 823, illustrated on page 109.

*(Author's illustration)*

Formed up also in mid-November 1942, this company was only eventually committed at the end of February 1943 in the fighting for Kharkov. Its losses were also only two Tigers for the whole of operations.

For Zitadelle, the unit which had in the meantime become the 9th s.SS-Pz.-Kp. had only fifteen Tigers. One of these was lost on the 7th July 1943 by a direct hit, the crew managing to escape. This was the only loss during the whole of Zitadelle. The Soviet offen-

sive at Kursk forced the retreating Germans towards Kharkov at the end of August 1943. The 9th company lost two new Tigers, scuttled at the end of July. The fighting carried on in the Alexeyewa-Stepanovka- Poltawa-Marijampol sectors until the Autumn of 1943.

The 9th company were the troubleshooters during the Winter of 1943-44 in the Petrowka-Bolschata-Wyka sectors and Alexeyewa.

By mid-April, the thirty initial Tigers had been lost

*Above.*
**The Tigers of the 9th s.Pz.- Kp. "Totenkopf" support the grenadiers of an infantry division during the retreat. The men seem shaken by the fighting.**
*(BZS)*

*Above right.*
**Unit markings of the "Totenkopf" division: the first sign used prior to Citadelle (top) and the sign used after that (bottom).**
*(Author's illustrations)*

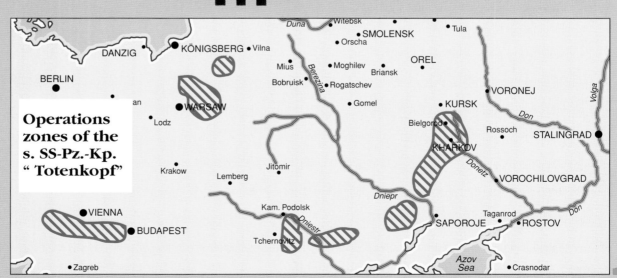

**Operations zones of the s. SS-Pz.-Kp. " Totenkopf"**

either in combat or scuttled as they could not be recovered. From May to July 1944, the unit received twenty-three Tigers in dribs and drabs, and fought with only a few machines in the Targul-Framos and Jassy sectors. From August to December, it was in the sector north-east of Warsaw. It had lost five Tigers in four months' fighting.

During the Winter of 1944-45, the company lost eight Tigers in just one week. At the end of March, there were only six tanks left. The final battles were to the south of Linz where the last two Tigers were scuttled. The troops surrendered to the Americans who handed them back to the Red Army. The Russians made them pay dearly for the loss of the last thousand-odd tanks destroyed by the unit during fifteen months of fighting. Few of them survived the prisoner of war camps.

In total the 4th and then the 9th company used about sixty Tigers. Despite lack of information on the unit, one may suppose that there were aces among its crews, the results obtained being something of an indication.

The s.Pz.- Abt. 103 (503) was created in the spring of 1944. After training on Tiger Is in Holland, then in Lithuania, it was sent to the south of Danzig, where it fought equipped with Tiger IIs. Subsequently, it took part in the fighting around Berlin. Two tank commanders, of whom one was *Obersturmführer* Körner, together destroyed sixty-four JS 2s and T 34s in a brief engagement (39 for Körner).

*Above.*
**The company commander's tank during the assault on Kharkov.**
*(BA)*

*Below.*
**423 showing the washed-out white camouflage.**
*(BA)*

A Tiger of the s.SS-Pz.-Kp. of the 3.SS-Panzergrenadier-Division "Totenkopf" in February 1943 in the Kharkov region. The use of the number 4 to designate the company of heavy tanks within two armoured SS divisions can lead to confusion. The

shape of the 4 is also the same as that used by the heavy company of the 1.SS-Panzergrenadier-Division. However, it is only possible to confuse the machines during the Winter seasons. Subsequently the colour of the number as well as the number itself changed. Another difference to be noted, was that the Tigers of the "Leibstandarte Adolf Hitler" rarely had smoke canisters at this period.
*(Author's illustration)*

*Above.*
**413 and behind, 431 in March 1943.**
*(WS)*

*Right.*
**For Operation Zitadelle, the company used the number 9 to indicate the 9th Kompanie. Here in the background, 933.**
*(BA)*

*Below.*
**911 with the light yellow base colour still visible.**
*(WS)*

*Below right.*
**Two Tigers on the way to the front, Summer 1943.**
*(KM)*

*Above.*
**Note the spare track links on the front of this Tiger. The situation is typical and represents the scene immediately behind the front-line.**
*(BA)*

*Above, right.*
**No. 913 is drawing up to the photograph, still followed by an Opel truck.**
*(BA)*

*Right.*
**Rail transport often meant changing the tracks. Note the tactical markings of the "Totenkopf": three bars.**
*(KM)*

*Below right.*
**Overhauling before the next assault.**
*(BA)*

119

*Above.*
**During the rear guard fighting after Zitadelle. The Tigers are heading towards the Mius sector, August 1943.**
*(KM)*

*Left.*
**The impacts on 921 are impressive. The crew hasn't lost its optimism. This was to change in a few months.**
*(BA)*

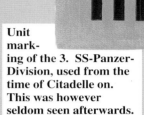

Unit marking of the 3. SS-Panzer-Division, used from the time of Citadelle on. This was however seldom seen afterwards.
*(Author's illustration)*

*Below.*
A Tiger of the heavy company of the 3.SS-Panzergrenadier-Division "Totenkopf" during the Battle of Kursk. The numbers that were painted white in the Spring were considered too visible. They were repainted a sand colour for Zitadelle, but preserved the black edging. The divisional sign, three vertical bars, was located near the radio operator/machine gunner's station. The smoke canisters and sometimes their supports were removed. The division had a lot of success at Kursk. On the 13th July 1943, it destroyed 61 tanks in 24 hours in the sector of Churawlinij. The Tigers claimed the majority.
*(Author's illustration)*

*Top left.*
**Autumn 1943. A few Tigers accompany the Panzer IVs of the division in the Krementshug sector.**
(BA)

*Above left.*
**912 covered in Zimmerit in Poland. Soon it would meet a much sterner foe.**
(BA)

*Above.*
**Well-known shot showing the uneven aspect of the Zimmerit. The photograph was taken in the northern sector of Warsaw. The unit participated in the operations against the insurrection.**
(BA)

*Left.*
**At Grafenwöhr, the new s.SS.-Pz.-Abt. 103 (503) training with out-of-date material like this Panzer III.**
(TA)

*Below.*
**A very interesting shot of a Pz I (VK 601), type C. What a difference with the Tigers I and II!**
*(TA)*

*Right.*
**Training accident or war wounds?**
*(TA)*

*Below.*
**This camouflage is remarkable for a Tiger. Note that the driving sprocket has been changed recently.**
*(TA)*

**Early formation sign of the " Totenkopf" Division .**
*(Author's illustration)*

*Right.*
**Machines moving across open country.**
*(TA)*

*Left.*
**Departure or arrival of a new machine. The Tiger uses standard tracks to drive aboard the flat car.**
*(TA)*

*Right.*
**Ad hoc hangars, typical of the Eastern front, are built at the training camp. Judging by the vegetation we are at the beginning of the Summer 1944.**
*(TA)*

*Below.*
**A brief break during the training.**
*(TA)*

*Right and below.*
**These two views are the last photos of the Tiger Is of the s.SS-Pz.-Abt. 103 (503), during the battalion's training in Holland.**
*(TA)*

*Below.*
**A Tiger of the heavy company of the 3.SS-Panzergrenadier-Division "Totenkopf". Until it became the s.SS.Pz.-Abt. 503, the company preserved its numbering system of white figures, here simply outlined directly on the camouflage pattern. Subsequently, on the Tiger IIs, the numbers were outlined with black paint. Although the battalion was less well-known, it was nonetheless formidable and fought to the last in Berlin.**
*(Author's illustration)*

# 12 - The 13th Schwere Kompani "Grossdeutschland" Division

Formed in January 1943, the 13th company fought for the first time during the offensive on Kharkov. The unit prepared itself for Operation Zitadelle where it fought for some time alongside with the Panthers of the 10th Pz.-Brigade without any Tigers lost.

At the beginning of August, it became the 9th company of the IIIrd (Armored) battalion of the Grossdeutschland Division.

In mid-August 1943, the unit was in the Achtyrka sector. The fighting took place in the sectors of Kirovograd and Tcherkassy, then in the Spring at Targul-Framos. The terrible Soviet offensive was particularly trying for the unit which fought against its first JS-2s in the Wirballen-Gumbinnen sectors. Little by little the numbers decreased and the last Tigers were lost in the Balga sector in March 1945.

During two year's campaigning, the unit lost a hundred-odd Tigers against 560 enemy tanks destroyed. Amongst its aces were *Feldwebel* Rempel, destroying, on one occasion, 18 T34s with a Tiger on its way to be repaired; and *Oblt* Beyer who scored 10 T-34 kills on 16th November 1943.

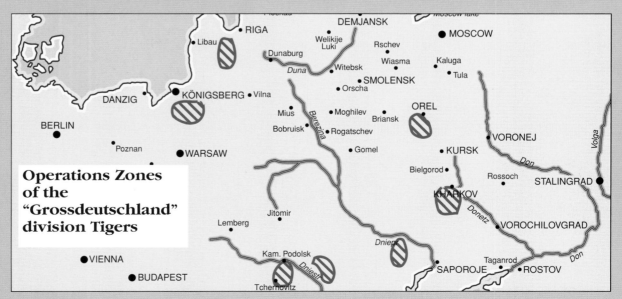

**Operations Zones of the "Grossdeutschland" division Tigers**

*Above.*
**No. 40 with an air-ground recognition flag, Winter 1943-44.**
*(ECPA)*

*Below.*
**The black massive shape of the Tiger stands out against the greyish-white of the countryside. The psychological effect must have been terrifying.**
*(ECPA)*

*Above.*
**A Tiger of the Heavy company of the Panzergrenadier-Division "Grossdeutschland" at the beginning of Winter 1943 in the Kharkov region. At this time, the tanks only had two numbers, which explains the confusion with the machines from the s.Pz-Abt. 505. Subsequently, the company camouflaged its Tigers with colours that matched those of the battleground. One part of the tanks delivered to the unit was painted grey, the other sand yellow.**
*(Author's illustration)*

*Right.*
**The S 20 seems to have been repainted in a lighter shade.**
*(BA)*

*Below.*
**The No. 20 is barely visible, painted in small figures on the turret. The machine is forging ahead in spite of the snow.**
*(ECPA)*

*Left.*
**General Manteuffel aboard his Kübel, with a Tiger in the background.**
*(BA)*

*Right.*
**Summer 1943, in the sector of Achtyrka. Tiger AO2 shows the first signs of combat. It belonged beforehand to the 13th company of the GD division.**
*(BA)*

WH-1405 592

A Tiger of the Heavy company of the Panzergrenadier-Division "Grossdeutschland" in the Kharkov area, March 1943. The machine is in sand yellow and the S on the turret has been patched over with the same colour. Curiously enough this tank has not been painted in white camouflage, maybe to help it to be recognised and not become a target for the PaKs.
(Author's illustration)

Top.
**The Tiger CO1 of the 11th company in September 1943 in the Dniepr sector.**
*(BA)*

Above.
**The BO1 of the 10th company passes in front of some divisional vehicles. The number of the SdKfz 251 is** *1540189.*
*(BA)*

Left.
**As the Tigers have radios, it's not a smoke signal!**
*(BA)*

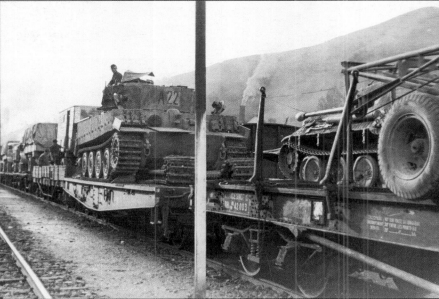

**Variations of the unit marking, on Panzer gray and sand yellow.**
*(Author's illustrations)*

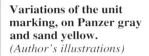

A Tiger of the 9th company of the III Abteilung of the "Grossdeutschland" Division during the fighting of the Winter of 1943-44 in the region of Kirovograd. The unit inflicted heavy losses on the 1st Front (General Vatutin) and the 2nd Ukrainian Front (General Koniev).
*(Author's illustration)*

133

*Left.*
**The commander of the 10th company aboard his Tiger B01.** *(WS)*

*Bottom.*
**A machine looking for a suitable place in order to trade its transport tracks for the wider combat tracks and install the mud guards.** *(BA)*

*Right.*
**In the Wilkowischen sector, Major Gomille's tank passes some 7.62cm Soviet cannon.** *(BA)*

*Opposite page, far right.*
**Under the captured guns lies an anti-tank rifle. These weapons were only effective against the tank tracks.** *(BA)*

*Opposite page, bottom.*
**Note the absence of camouflage on BO1 as well as the sloping figures.** *(BA)*

*Below.*

**A Tiger of the 11th company of the III Abteilung of the "Grossdeutschland" Division during August and September 1943 in the region of Achtyrka-Kharkov-Poltava. The Tigers covered the German retreat towards the new lines of defence on the Dniepr. After the heavy losses at Kursk, the Soviets again lost 1 864 tanks from the 3rd to the 23rd August 1943, which were to be added to the 4 500 tanks lost during offensive and defensive operations at Kursk and Orel. In July, the Germans lost 645 tanks, and in the following month 572 of which 73 Tigers, on both fronts combined (west and east).**

*(Author's illustration)*

*Above.*
**B12 in complete camouflage and spare track links on the front plate.**
*(BA)*

*Right.*
**An interesting view showing Tiger C33 from the 11th company.**
*(BA)*

*Below.*
**The 9th company commander's tank. The machine appears to have suffered a lot and seems to be used here as an artillery piece.**
*(BZS)*

*Left.*
A very geometric camouflage pattern for these Tigers. In the background, a damaged Panther.
*(WS)*

*Below.*
The last photographs before the end are very rare...
*(WS)*

*Below left.*
...However, this one shows several Panzers, including a Tiger of the GD, apparently abandoned in a German town. The Tiger is at the front right ; note the open driver's hatch.
*(KM)*

*Below.*
The Tiger of *Hauptmann* Villebois, commander of the 10th company of the III Abteilung of the "Grossdeutschland" Division. In July 1944, the unit faced the great Soviet onslaught on the East Prussian frontier, in the region of Wilkowischken-Tilsitt. The Tigers confronted the new super-heavy Stalin 2 tanks, and the engagements did not always turn to their advantage. On the 6th August 1944, four Tigers were lost during fighting for Hill 51. The battle was pursued in order to save several bridgeheads. On the 20th March 1945, the last two Tigers (*Unteroffiziere* Feuerpfeil and Kroneis) made their gallant last stand near Königsberg.
*(Author's illustration)*

## Other units equipped with the Tiger I

Other units were equipped with the Tiger I, among which the Pz-Korps "Hermann Göring". Dealing with this unit would be well beyond the scope of this study. The works of Wolfgang Schneider, whose *Tiger in combat*, volume two, has just been released, are strongly recommended.

# Conclusion

The Tiger I played a role of capital importance during the conflict. Its appearance on the front, going some way to balancing things for the Germans, prolonged the Nazi regime's death throes, and delayed its collapse. Compared with any other Allied tank of the period the Tiger was undeniably superior. This would explain the amazing scores of the 502, 503, and 505 s.Pz-Abteilungen. The 501 and 504 s.Pz-Abt. also scored an impressive tally in North Africa, but this has often been minimised by Allied propaganda or by a lack of knowledge on the part of contemporary historians.

The new units that were engaged from the middle of 1943 and at the beginning of 1944 did experience difficulties when taking on the new generations of Soviet tanks and anti-tank weapons. However, even when confronted with its most fearsome opponent, the JS 2, the Tiger came out on top. Its powerful quick-firing cannon, which fired a combined shell and cartridge, was a major advantage since the JS 2 used a shell whose charge was separate. A fight between JS 2s and Tigers of the 3/507 s.Pz-Abt on the 12 January 1945 ended with with twenty-two JS 2s destroyed.

Without loss, the Tigers destroyed the Rus-

*Above.*
**A Tiger commander of the s.Pz-Abt. 502, in the Leningrad sector, Winter 1943-44.**
*(BA)*

sian tanks in a few moments. As far as armour is concerned, the two tanks were the same, although the JS 2 had a much better profile than the Tiger.

The other determining advantage of the Tigers was the intensive training of their elite crews, who were all volunteers and veterans of previous campaigns.

It was during the Battle of Kursk, from 4th July to 23 August 1943, that the Tiger showed its mettle. This battle was a real duck shoot for the s.Pz-Abt. and the s.Pz-Kompanie which were engaged with minimal losses. The s.Pz-Abt.503 and 505 counted three Tigers lost each during Operation Zitadelle and thirteen others during the Soviet offensive. In other words, nineteen Tigers des-

*Left.*
**The tank commander's seat in the turret.**
*(BA)*

*Right.*
**A Tiger being resupplied with shells during the Battle of Kursk.**
*(WS)*

troyed during the fifty days of the Battle of Kursk. The 503 and 505 are the two largest Tiger battalions, alone accounting for almost two-thirds of the Tigers committed at Kursk. This is a far cry from the hundreds and hundreds of Tigers apparently lost at Kursk.

But it wasn't enough to command a Tiger to be able to claim to be an "ace". Some crews didn't score during the conflict, losing their Tigers for mechanical reasons, running out of fuel or being destroyed by enemy fire. Others set too much store on the strength of some bridges... luck remained the real master of the field.

The amazing scores on the Eastern front can also be explained by the bad weather. Cursed at the beginning of the campaign, it

*Right.*
**The loader's position, who also mans the coaxial machine gun.** *(BA)*

*Above.*
**His battle station. In real conditions, the hatch would be shut.**
*(BA)*

*Below.*
**The driver's seat.**
*(BA)*

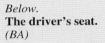

became the armour's principal ally for it prevented the Soviet Air Force from operating freely. This was not the case on the Western front where the German armour was continually harassed.

The big disadvantage of the Tiger was the under-powered engine (642 hp for the first series, subsequently increased slightly to 694 hp) which only gave 10.5 hp/tonne and 12.3 hp /tonne. Transportation problems and the huge fuel consumption rate added to this. This did not however discourage the Germans from continuing the race for the biggest machine, with the Tiger II and its off-shoot the Jagdtiger, respectively 68 and 70 tonnes, and above all the famous Maus.

The Krupp design bureau's Maus project

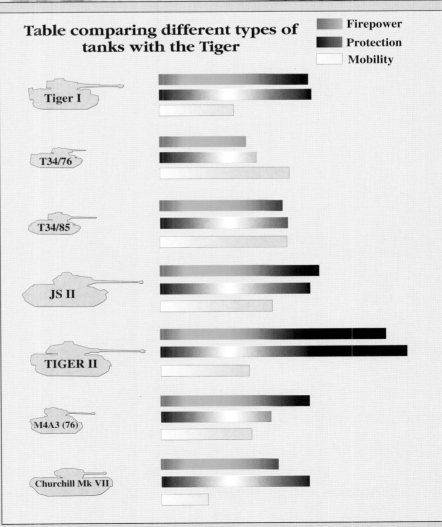

**Table comparing different types of tanks with the Tiger**

Firepower
Protection
Mobility

Tiger I

T34/76

T34/85

JS II

TIGER II

M4A3 (76)

Churchill Mk VII

139

*Above.*
**Maintenance at the repair workshop of the "Grossdeutschland".**
*(WS)*

*Below.*
**The turret has been lifted, revealing the leverage system. In the front, did the horseshoe bring luck to this crew from s.Pz-Abt. 505?**
*(BZS)*

went back to 1941. Its development was given to Porsche in March 1942 and the 188 tonne "baby" made its first trials on 24th December 1943. It had one Kwk 44 12.8 cm cannon and one Kwk 44 7.5cm cannon, its armour-plating was 240mm thick at its thickest on the front and 180-200 on the sides. In spite of its size, this bunker-on-tracks was easy to drive and was very mobile. It was only the fuel consumption which presented a problem in these years of scarcity - 0.202 miles per gallon!

If the Tiger crews' brilliant actions, their adversaries, obsessions and skills are often recounted, the efforts of the mechanics, who often got a machine ready overnight so that it could fight the enemy the next day were incredible. These men, like all mechanics, worked real miracles, often using rudimentary equipment or risking their lives recovering a broken-down tank in open country. They were the sole insurance for the tank crews. A good team meant a reliable tank which meant one more chance of being victorious. It was also to these men that the aces owed their amazing scores.

The thousand-odd Tigers used on the Eastern front destroyed more than 8 000 ene-

*Above.*
**A specialist at work on a Tiger of s.Pz-Abt. 503.**
*(BZS)*

*Right.*
**With the turret removed, the vital parts of the Tiger were accessible.**
*(BZS)*

*Below.*
**Changing a gun barrel on a 9.SS-s.Pz-Kp "Totenkopf" Tiger. The leverage point can be seen on the turret side.**
*(BA)*

my armour. These figures are sufficient proof of this tank's worth and no other tank can be compared to it. And even if the construction design was already out of date from 1944 onwards, the results obtained proved that theories were wrong.

*Above*
**The turret is merely balanced on beams and petrol barrels.**
*(BA)*

*Left.*
**The same view as on previous page from a different angle. Poland, end 1944.**
*(BA)*

*Above.*
**The engine of a Tiger from the 13.s.SS-Pz-Kp "Leibstandarte Adolf Hitler".**
*(BZS)*

*Below.*
**The crane was able to lift 16 tonnes, as can be read on the sign.**
*(BA)*

*Opposite page, top.*
**The two wheel sprockets have been removed, revealing a lot of technical details.**
*(BA)*

*Opposite page.*
**Apart from maintaining the machines, the mechanics must remove the marks left by the impacts of shells...**
*(BZS)*

*Opposite page, bottom.*
**... And this sometimes poses problems which are difficult to solve.**
*(WS)*

# THE TIGER I'S ROAD WHEELS

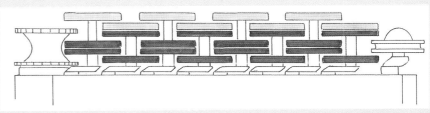

## 1. Transport
In order to transport the Tiger by rail, sixteen road wheels (in grey) had to be taken off as well as the tracks. This operation took a lot of time and delayed the tank's combat-readiness. Figure 1 shows the dismantling necessary for only one side of the tank.

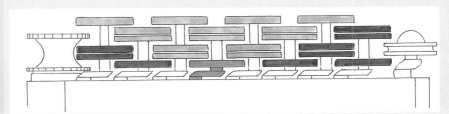

## 2. Repairs
In the event of the destruction of a wheel on the rear row or even a torsion bar (in red), nearly fourteen wheels had to be removed (in grey), a huge job in bad weather.

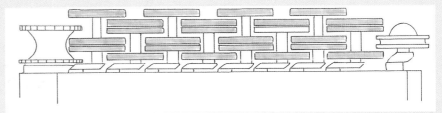

## 3. Protection
One of the advantages of torsion-bar suspension was the braking effect in the case of a direct hit on the road wheels, as the shell nearly always burst before it reached the tank's hull.

*Left.*
**This photograph, although of poor quality, is interesting as it shows a Tiger, in Winter 1944 still equipped with Feiffel filters.**
*(DR)*

*Right.*
**The caption on this Soviet photograph explains that hundreds of Tigers suffered the same fate as this one at Kursk. As only 147 Tigers were committed in this battle, there is no need to comment.**
*(DR)*

*Below.*
**The end of the road for this Tiger of s.Pz-Abt. 506 in Summer 1944. The number *308* has been painted on by the Red Army and this tank is captioned as having been destroyed or captured in 'sector A'.**
*(DR)*

## Acknowledgements

I should like to thank my wife Nicole, for her understanding and her patience, in spite of long working days turning into working nights; my principal friends who contributed their photos, information and advice and helped realise this book. I should like to mention Messrs Gérard Gorokhoff, Karl-Heinz Münch, Thomas Anderson and last but not least, Wolfgang Schneider.

I wish to thank also MM. Guglielmi, Peyrani and F. von Rosen for the additional informations they have brought, which have been duly included in this third print.

**Photo credits.** Bundesarchiv *(BA)*, Thomas Anderson *(TA)*, E.C.P.Armées *(ECPA)*, Imperial War Museum *(IWM)*, Karl-Heinz Münch *(KM)*, Wolfgang Schneider *(WS)*, Bundes Zeitgenossichte Archiv, Stuttgart *(BZS)*.

**Bibliography:**
– The best book on the subject is *Tiger in combat, vol. I,* by W. Schneider. The second volume has just been released;
– *Tiger in the Mud,* Otto Carius;
– The individual Tiger Unit Histories which have come out since the end of the conflict, especially those of the 503 and 507 s.Pz-Abt.;
– The excellent book by Patrick Agde : *Michaël Wittmann*;
– The Story of the Leibstandarte;
– *Division Das Reich*, Otto Weidinger;
– *Soldaten, Kämpfe, Kamerad* (Totenkopf);
– *Wie ein Fels in Meer* (Totenkopf);
– and all the histories of the various infantry and armour divisions that are too numerous to list out here.

ISBN : 2-908182-81-5

Publisher's number : 2-908182

*1st printing © Histoire & Collections 1999*

*2nd printing © Histoire & Collections 2001*

*3rd printing © Histoire & Collections 2003*

**Histoire & Collections**
SA au capital de 182 938,82 €

5, avenue de la République
F-75541 Paris Cédex 11 - France

Telephone : (33)1 40 21 18 20
Fax : (33)1 47 00 51 11

This book has been designed, typed, laid-out and processed by Histoire & Collections, fully on integrated computer equipment.
Supervision and layout by Philippe Charbonnier
Translated from the French by Alan McKay
Cover design by the author and Patrick Lesieur
Text typed by Sylvaine Noël
Maps by Morgan Gillard
Color separation by FRT Graphic
Printed by Zure, Spain
European Union. *February 2003*